ISRAEL WAY



# Full-Time PARENTING

## A Guide to Family-Based Discipleship

# Full-Time Parenting:
# A Guide to Family-Based Discipleship

by Israel Wayne

*Address all inquiries and comments to:*

Wisdom's Gate Ministries
www.WisdomsGate.org
800-343-1943
wisgate@wisgate.com

Wisdom's Gate Ministries ©2012
First Formal Printing
ISBN-10: 0-9728139-5-0
ISBN-13: 978-0-9708139-5-2

# FULL-TIME PARENTING

*by Israel Wayne*

# DEDICATION

*This book is dedicated to the many mentors and examples with whom I have been blessed in my life. I have learned from watching your marriages and the kind and gracious ways that you interact with your children.*

*To my grandparents, who delight in their great-grandchildren.*

*To my mother, who was the epitome of Full-Time Parenting. I'm standing on your shoulders. Thank you for laying such a sure foundation.*

*To my sisters, who I love.*

*To my dear sweet wife, Brook, who loves me in spite of myself. You are a wonderful wife and mother. I couldn't be more blessed!*

*To my sweet children. You are the best part of my life. I promise to do everything in my power to introduce you to the Lord Jesus Christ whom I have come to know and love. My heart's desire is to see you walking in Truth. I love you each with all of my heart.*

*Thank you to Virginia Youmans for her help on the manuscript. Thank you to my friends Scott Somerville, Michael P. Donnelly and Bradley Pierce for wise counsel and advice.*

# INTRODUCTION

Once your first child is born and you hold that helpless bundle in your arms, life suddenly takes on a new level of importance. You have been entrusted with an eternal soul that will live forever, either in God's presence, or in eternal separation from Him.

What you do now, as a parent, will have a dramatic impact not only on the life of your child, but on his or her eternity as well.

Because of the importance of this Godly calling, many parents have chosen to embrace what I call "Full-Time Parenting." Parents who choose to be a Full-Time Parenting team desire to take as much responsibility for the care and upbringing of their children as they possibly can. They don't want to outsource the raising of their child to someone else. They aren't looking for ways to shirk their duties or pawn off their children to another. They not only see a need to be involved full-time in their child's life, they *want* to be involved. This is because they love their child and want the best for him or her.

Instead of viewing parenting primarily as providing for the physical needs of the child (as important as that is!), they see it as their God-ordained mandate to provide for their children emotionally and spiritually as well.

*Full-Time Parenting* is NOT necessarily a book about being a stay-at-home parent, living on one income, or being a single parent (although it will address each of these issues).

Full-Time Parents look for every opportunity to teach and train their children in the ways of the Lord, just as they are commanded in Deuteronomy 6. They teach them when they rise up in the morning, when they sit in their home, when they leave their home, and when they lie down at night. They don't want to let a single opportunity slip by without being able to impart important eternal truths to their child.

If that sounds like you, then I invite you to join with me as we explore this Full-Time Parenting journey in the chapters of this book.

**"Parenting is NOT about producing some kind of predictable Pavlovian or Skinnerian behavior from our children. We are not training them like laboratory rats to respond to positive or negative stimuli. Our desire is that we have our children's hearts."**

CHAPTER

1

# BE THE PARENT

*"Lo, children are an heritage of the Lord: and the fruit of the womb is his reward."*
(Psalm 127:3)

ON THE ONE HAND, parenting is the most difficult task you will ever undertake. If you think you are equipped to be a good parent, think again. You aren't. You are in over your head. You have been given a task that is beyond your means and abilities. So that's the bad news.

The good news, on the other hand, is that you are not alone. The God of the Universe, Who placed these precious children into your hands and home, is in covenant partnership with you in the raising of these children. Actually, Biblically speaking, these children belong to Him (Psalm 127), and He rewards us by allowing us to be caretakers and stewards of HIS children. Because they don't belong to you, but to Him, you need to find out what He expects of you and how He wants you to raise His children.

You can't just do any old thing you like. You can't simply treat them any way you want to, or spend only as much time parenting as you want to, or send them to any old school you want to. You need to find out what God's desire is for these children. How does HE want HIS children to be raised?

The good thing is that He is not silent. He has given us a wealth of knowledge and direction in His Word about parenting, education, and child training. As partners with Him in the raising of His children, He doesn't expect us to be perfect parents. He *does*, however, expect us to give 100% of our heart to this process. If we look to Him, God will give us wisdom and understanding about how to do this job in a way that pleases Him (James 1:5).

**Basic Ground Rules**

There are a few basic guidelines that will make a host of difference in terms of your effectiveness in being a good parent.

*You Are the Parent, They Are the Children*

It's alarming how many Christian parents haven't figured out this basic premise. They have a three-year-old who runs the house, and the parents live in abject frustration because of the tyranny of a child they cannot control.

Before any of our children were born, I told my wife, "Whenever our children decide to defy our authority and challenge our position as their parents, I am committed, by the grace of God, that they will lose—every single time. We will ensure that they understand that it is not in their best interests to try to rule the home." To the best of my knowledge, we've stuck to that promise. I don't know of a single case, with any of our children, when they won a contest of the wills.

To say that achieving such a goal is hard is the understatement of the century! You need to plan on investing *huge* sums of time into parenting if you want to establish a clear understanding in your child's mind regarding who is in charge. However, just having this ground rule in place *before* our children were born made a huge difference in how we approached parenting. Letting the child "win" the authority battle is simply not an option—ever. It makes parenting much easier once it is clear in your own mind just who is in charge.

Someone asked me recently if we have ever had a strong-willed child. I replied, "Yes, all of them." While I understand that some children are far more naturally defiant than others, *all* children want to get their own way. Every child who has ever been born has a strong will; they just express their wills in different ways.

Too many parents want so badly to be liked by their children. Here's the deal—children don't respect parents who are afraid of them (and therefore they don't like them much either). Don't make being your child's buddy your chief goal. Be the parent. Be firm and consistent. There are plenty of ways to have fun, show love, cuddle with, read to, and be a blessing to your children without letting them run over top of you. When you give them an instruction, they don't have to *like* it. They just need to *do* it. Once they get that through their heads, and they know that disobedience and defiance is *never* an option, they will settle in and enjoy life.

*Children Need Boundaries*

Children can't handle having unlimited possibilities. Children thrive on security, predictability, order, structure, and boundaries, not on chaos and randomness. Some parents think they are stifling their children's creativity or "free spirit" by creating rules and boundaries for them. Nonsense. The greatest creativity always flows from structure. Great concert pianists who have the greatest ease, and whose fingers float effortlessly over the ivories, are the ones who have spent thousands of painstaking hours learning the form and intricate methods of music theory. The truly great painters produce masterpieces because of how well they understand the geometry of art and obey the rules of symmetry.

To a great extent, children should have schedules. Structure can, of course, be overdone, and we've all met parents who need to learn to lighten up a bit and let their children be children. But in general, children need to have basic times when they get up in the morning, when they go to sleep, when they eat, and when their do their studies. They need to know what Mom and Dad expect from them. They need to have predictable consequences if they are lazy, sloppy, disobedient, mean to a sibling, or back-talk their parents. They can't handle a situation where Mom deals with things one way and Dad deals with them in an opposite way. They can't makes sense of random punishments where Mom flies off the handle for something on Tuesday, ignores the same offense on Wednesday, and has a completely different reaction on Thursday for the same misbehavior.

Children feel a tremendous sense of security from knowing that Mom and Dad love them, that they love each other, that they are safe, that they will be provided for, that their parents love them enough to tell them no (and mean it!) and follow through with appropriate consequences if they disobey.

*Value Your Words*

Do your words mean anything to you? They should. If you give your child an instruction, value your own words to them. If you don't really intend for your child to make his bed, then don't bother telling him to do it, just make it yourself. However, if you actually, really, genuinely *want* your son to make his *own bed*, then you had better value your words enough to make sure that it happens. Provide some guidelines so your son knows *when* he is supposed to accomplish this (i.e., "You need to have your bed made in the next fifteen minutes before breakfast"), give a predictable consequence if it doesn't happen, and then follow through with it as necessary.

If I am giving my son an instruction, I will usually do the following: I will say, "Son, I need you to go outside and pick up all of the whiffle balls and put them away. Do you understand?"

"OK."

"Good. What do I want you to do?"

"I don't know." (He wasn't really listening. I tell him again.)

"You want me to pick up all the whiffle balls in the yard and put them away."

"Correct. Do it right away."

"Yes, sir."

We always require our children to say, "Yes, sir," or "Yes, ma'am," when they are given an instruction. It lets us know they are attentive and responsive. (If that sounds too formal for you, use whatever you are comfortable with.) When they fail to answer appropriately, or with an appropriate tone of voice, it usually indicates that they are having a sour attitude and that their hearts are not with us. We then address the attitude before returning to the instruction at hand.

*Train Their Hearts, Not Just Their Behavior*

Parenting is *not* about producing some kind of predictable Pavlovian or Skinnerian behavior from our children. We are not training them like laboratory rats to respond to positive or negative stimuli. Our desire is that we have our children's hearts. We want them to be fully participating on the family team.

Successful Full-Time Parenting is not the Marines. It is not about children dutifully saying "Yes, ma'am," and obeying barked-out orders, yet hating their parents in their hearts. Anger, bitter words, deceit, meanness, sulking, pouting, complaining, etc., are all works of the flesh (see Galatians 5). We want our children to learn how to walk in the Spirit. Our goal is to raise children who love God (and their parents) from their hearts. We want them to have a dynamic relationship with God (and with us) and to serve out of a heart of love, not out of mere duty and obligation. If they don't "feel the love" at a given moment, that's okay. They can just obey anyway and wait for the warm fuzzies to come back later. The main thing, though, is that we are reaching their hearts. We are helping them to live servant-hearted lives. We are training them to think not of themselves only, but of the needs of others (1 Peter 4:10).

*Have a Goal*

You need to know why you are parenting. Thirty years from now, what will define success for you, as a parent? How will you know if you have accomplished your goals if they aren't clear in your own mind? Do you know why you are raising your children? Is it simply so they can get good grades, go to college, have careers, pay the bills, retire, move to Florida, and die?

What kind of persons do you hope they will become? How do you hope they will teach and train your grandchildren? Personally, I think the true success of my parenting will be evidenced in the lives of my great-grandchildren. If my children's children are discipling *their* children well, then I will feel like a success. I cover more of the big-picture goals for parenting in the chapter, "The Father's Role."

*Throw Yourself on the Mercy of God*

One of my great heroes of the faith is a 19th-century Dutch missionary to South Africa named Andrew Murray. Andrew Murray wrote many wonderful books, including: The Believer's Absolute Surrender; With Christ in the School of Prayer; Holiness; With Christ in the School of Obedience; Abiding in Christ, and many others. He and his wife Emma were Godly parents of eight children who all grew up serving the Lord as missionaries or pastors (or as wives of missionaries or pastors).

In his book on parenting, *Raising Your Children to Love Christ*, Murray talks about our inadequacies as parents. I will summarize some of his thoughts for you. He says that as a parent you want to teach, train, disciple, correct, instruct, challenge, rebuke, encourage, praise, and lead your child. You do absolutely everything you can to help this child know and love God. At the end of it all, however, there are some things that you just can't do for your child. You need to do everything you can to keep your end of the covenant with God in this child-raising process. However, doing the best you can do is not enough. Your best efforts will still fall short. You are an imperfect parent, and you will make mistakes.

So what do you do? Give up? Admit defeat? No, not at all! Remember that God loves HIS children more than you ever could, and that He has so much invested in them. If you have done everything you can, to the best of your ability, then throw yourself on the mercy of God and plead for Him to make up for your lack. Cry out to God and ask Him to do in your child's heart and mind what you cannot accomplish. Ask Him to create circumstances that will direct this child to surrendering his or her life to Christ.

When you do this, do it with a full heart of confidence, knowing that God will move heaven and earth to keep His part of the covenant, if you have been faithful in your part. You are not alone in this parenting process. You are not even the most important component. The Spirit of the living God is also at work, and you are in partnership with that Spirit. Look to Christ at every turn. Seek Him and His wisdom daily. Turn to Him and let Him lead you, every step of the journey. You can't do this alone, but the good news is, you aren't expected to!

CHAPTER

# 2

# HOW I TAUGHT MY CHILDREN TO SIT STILL AND BE QUIET

*"Be still, and know that I am God."*
(Ps. 46:10a)

When my wife and I were first married we invited a family to our house for a visit. They had seven children, ages one to 14, who were all homeschooled. We all sat together in our living room for three hours enjoying fellowship and conversation. I was amazed by their children for several reasons.

First of all, they sat quietly without getting up and running around for *three hours*! I had never seen children do this. At first, I would have suspected that perhaps this was abnormal and unhealthy—something that shouldn't be encouraged—until I realized that they were all *enjoying* listening to the conversation!

The second thing that surprised me was that they did not interrupt the adult conversation but were content to listen rather than talk and share their own thoughts and ideas. Again, I would have thought that perhaps they were just socially inept and that they didn't *know how* to communicate, until their parents would ask them to share something, or when my wife and I asked them a question. Then they would smile and speak up in a clear and appropriately loud voice to answer our question, and then sometimes they would ask us a question in return. They were truly interested in other people.

Even though I did not yet have children, I knew that I must learn the secret of how one family could raise a houseful of well-mannered, respectful, appropriately quiet, and pleasantly conversant children. To this day, I have not met a family that lives in such peace and harmony with each other and with others. So, I asked them how they did it. Their answer was not at all what I would have suspected.

**Positive Socialization**

Their first secret, they informed me (rather tongue-in-cheek), was to keep their children away from other children! This seemed so contrary to all of the parenting advice in books and articles by "parenting experts." They said that their children were not permitted to spend time alone with other children their own age, but that their family always interacted with other families as a family unit, rather than as individuals. So they did have interaction with other children, but it was always in a supervised context with their parents present to provide careful oversight.

**The Simple Life**

Secondly, they did not permit their children to watch television or play video games. They did not listen to aggressive music or play foolish games, so they had lots of time to do real work with their hands (planting a garden, carrying firewood, etc.), or enjoy reading a book together as a family. They lived a very simple life in a simple house, with very little clutter. I once asked them how they could fit nine people so comfortably into such a small house, and they answered that they didn't want a larger house because then they would just accumulate more stuff. They wanted life to be basic and simple. That is so unlike most families.

**Proper Nutrition**

Third, they completely eliminated sugar and caffeine from their diets. This made a lot of sense to me. It is completely unfair to give children substances that pump them up and make them hyper and then expect them to sit still and be quiet. Make it easier for them and yourself by giving them a good wholesome diet.

**Daily Family Worship**

Fourth, they had a time of family worship every morning before the father went to work (he has a workshop on his own property so that if the children need attention or direction during the day he is available). They explained that they would read the word of God and have a time of singing and prayer each and every morning. Every child was present and was expected to be still. All of the children who were old enough would sit on a chair or on the couch, and the baby would be held by his mother. They would begin this process from birth, so the children never thought it was strange. They would also read books together as a family at night, so they had even more practice sitting still and listening.

**An Incremental Process**

As you might expect, my wife and I began to implement many of these principles with our own children as they came along. I doubt that we have done any of these things as a well as our friends (especially eliminating clutter!), but we have seen very good fruit from these practices in our children.

For families who have not done this with their children from birth, I would suggest that you ease into the process. Start with five minutes a day total. Then work up to ten, and then fifteen. Eventually your children will easily sit still for an hour or more. You can read the Bible for five minutes, sing for ten (this is something in which they are participating, so they are less likely to get bored), and then have short time of prayer. Our family usually meets from a half an hour to an hour every morning. We try to read a chapter from the Bible each day. (Of course, we also discuss in depth what we are reading, so sometimes our progress is a bit slow.) A certain amount of predictability and structure is required so the children know what to expect, but the parents can feel a great liberty to do what they feel is best for each morning meeting.

**Start Young**

There is usually a bit of resistance that is expressed once a child reaches the toddler years. Once a baby can crawl, he usually would rather be on the floor moving around than sitting on Mama's lap. There will be plenty of time for that during the day, but not during "Bible time." This is a time to sit still and be quiet. Not only does this teach the child self-control and good listening habits, but most importantly, it gives him a necessary foundation of knowing and understanding the Word of God.

For a child who is around one year old, simply holding the child on your lap and restraining him when he wants to get down may be sufficient. He will probably cry and fuss at first, which makes it hard for the other children to hear the Bible lesson, but that is okay. Remember that training, rather than merely getting through a lesson, is one of the primary objective here. When the child gets a bit older, say 1½ to four years old, he will probably give you some resistance to sitting still and being quiet. You may need to take a moment away from the lesson to give the child a loving and appropriate discipline, and then bring him back to sit down again. You won't win this battle in a day, or even in a month. You will win it by doing it every day, day after day, week after week for years, until the child is a teenager. Then, as I have observed in other families who practice this, he can begin to contribute very meaningfully by sharing with the rest of the family the things the Lord is teaching him from the family lesson, or his own personal Bible study time.





**A Day in Our Life**

We've had days where it seemed that all we did was train our children and we couldn't even finish reading the selected Bible passage. That is okay. We don't get upset about it. We are meeting our goals and objectives. Our children are learning to sit still, listen and be obedient. The purpose of sitting still and listening is to give your children the tools they need (self-discipline) to be able to learn and be successful in life.

During our Bible time, we want our children to ask questions if there is anything they don't understand. It is designed to be interactive and I try to draw out each child to seek their participation in answering questions, and demonstrating that they have understood what we have studied. Usually by age five or so, we are seeing remarkable progress in our child's abilities to be still and listen to adult conversations.

We have a personal preference to have our children with us during church meetings, rather than having them sent to age-segregated Sunday schools or "Junior Church." Most families cannot have their children sit with them during the entire service, even if they wanted to, because the children will not be quiet and obedient that long. The key for us has been to practice every day at home.

For me, Bible time works best in the morning before I leave for work. For some families it works best at night, after dinner (or some other time of the day). There isn't a right or wrong to this; the main thing is to make sure you are consistent. We like to read books in the evenings, or sometimes watch an educational video at night as a family. Whatever works for your family is great; use the tine to instill the right kind of values into your children and teach them self-control.

### Learning Social Skills

Regarding positive social interaction with adults and other children, your children will need practice. My wife works with our children to practice shaking someone's hand, look them in the eye, speak up in an appropriately loud and clear voice, and be genuinely interested in other people, and not just themselves. We still have a long way to go in these areas, but we are seeing slow progress.

### A Long Obedience in the Same Direction

As I always tell my wife, "Parenting is a marathon, not a sprint. We win by being consistent day after day for years. Parenting is very, very easy. We just need do all of the right things every day from the time that our child is born until he turns twenty, and everything will turn out great!" Those last two lines always get a look from my wife that says, "That doesn't sound easy to me!" The fact is it isn't easy. There are lots of trials and errors, failures and successes, but in the long run you do see good fruit from a "long obedience in the same direction."

### Dad Should Lead

This daily training is something that is ideally the father's responsibility, and he should be leading this effort. Men, it is not your wife's job to train your children, it is your job. She is your helpmeet, not the other way around. You need to take the time to invest in your children.

### When Dad Can't or Won't Lead

For a wife who has a husband who is unable to lead his family in daily Scripture study and worship (perhaps because of unique work requirement where he is gone for days on end), or who is unsaved, or who is just unwilling to lead in family worship, much of this training can be done by the wife. It is never ideal to have only one parent involved in this daily training. I know that neither my wife nor I could do it very well alone, but if necessary, we each would do it individually. It is of primary importance to us. A single parent can lead family worship alone if they have no spouse to help.

I would advise a wife to share this chapter with her husband and ask him to lead the family in daily family worship. If he will not, then do not nag your husband. You, as the sanctifying spouse, can be an agent of grace to your children. When your husband is gone, gather your children for singing, Bible reading, and prayer. Don't make it an event that everyone hates. Keep it moving and keep the lessons short, especially at first. If you don't know what you are doing, that's okay; most of the rest of us don't either. If you have never had family worship modeled for you, that's okay; most of the rest of us haven't either. The good news is, your children will have it modeled for them, and it will be much easier for them when it is their turn to become parents.

**A Time and Place for Everything**

It is not *always* important for children to sit still and be quiet. They are children and should be allowed to play, have fun, and be noisy. We don't want them to be miserable during their whole childhood. But they do need to learn how to quiet down and behave appropriately in certain situations. You don't want them acting up at a funeral, or a wedding, or a church service, or when guests have come over for dinner. There is a time and place for being rowdy, and then there is a time to be silent and respectful. There is a time for every purpose under Heaven.

**Parenting is a Marathon, Not a Sprint**

Don't expect short-term gains. This is a long-term project. You may not notice much improvement in your children for weeks, or months, or maybe even a couple of years. That's okay. Just keep being faithful. God will reward your diligence over time. Remember also that this is not merely about obeying rules and being legalistic, but rather about passing on your heart and love for the Lord to your children. They will rise to meet your own love and worship of the Savior. You are leading, they are following. Make sure that your own heart is clean and pure before the Lord and that you are not simply following a rigid duty, but that you are doing this from a heart of love. This is not about trying to look good on the outside. May the Lord grant you wisdom and grace as you pursue these changes.

CHAPTER

# 3

# THE SEVEN-YEAR TEACHING METHOD

*"At the end of every seven years ... gather the people together ... that they may hear, and learn, and fear the Lord your God."* (Deuteronomy 31:10-13)

NOT LONG AGO I was talking with a friend of mine who is a Full-Time Parent of eleven children. To maintain a close relationship with his children, he often takes a child with him when he makes deliveries for his business. He told me about an experience he recently had with his seven-year-old daughter.

They had to wait a few minutes in the truck before unloading, so he grabbed his pocket Bible and began to read to his daughter. Shortly after he began reading he became aware that his daughter was not familiar with the story. This surprised my friend, who was certain that he would have told his daughter this well-known account in Scripture. His older children knew the story, and he reads the Bible regularly to all of his children, so how could his seven-year-old have missed this?

He was reminded of the Scripture in Deuteronomy 31 in which God instructed all His people, from oldest to youngest, to review His entire law.

*"And Moses commanded them, saying, 'At the end of every seven years, in the solemnity of the year of release, in the feast of tabernacles, When all Israel is come to appear before the Lord thy God in the place which he shall choose, thou shalt read this law before all Israel in their hearing. Gather the people together, men, and women, and children, and thy stranger that is within thy gates, that they may hear, and that they may learn, and fear the Lord your God, and observe to do all the words of this law: And that their children, which have not known any thing, may hear, and learn to fear the Lord your God, as long as ye live in the land whither ye go over Jordan to possess it'"* (Deut. 31:10-13, KJV).

### My Own Experience

As I contemplated this passage, I reflected on my own life. When I was seven I knew all of the major Bible stories and wanted people to know that I was a Christian. I was the quizzing champ at our Sunday School and won prizes for memorization at Vacation Bible School. I believed the Bible to be true and wanted to obey God.

Seven years later, at age fourteen, I was faced with an entirely different set of circumstances in life. I was dealing with peer pressure, struggling with dating issues, transitioning into manhood, wrestling with being submitted to authority, learning about conformity, popularity, and fitting in, etc. My relationship with God was at a real turning point.

At twenty-one, my world had changed again. As a single young man I was in the middle of national ministry, waiting on God to bring me a wife in His timing, and past the turmoil of the teen years. God had been merciful to me in allowing me to be discipled by loving brothers and sisters who helped to demonstrate a Godly lifestyle for me and to shape my worldview. I was at rest, enjoying life, and serving the Lord.

At twenty-eight, I was happily married, a father of three sweet children, and I had learned a lot about myself. I was trying to balance the demands of work and ministry with investing properly in my wife and children. I was learning how to put into practice all of the things I had been taught as a child about life and family.

When I was seven I wanted to avoid getting into trouble, when I was fourteen I wanted to fit in, when I was twenty-one I wanted direction for my life, and at twenty-eight ... I wanted a nap.

### Teaching Our Children

I have observed that Christian parents often do a decent job of training their older children, but they slack off with their later ones. I guess they get tired, or perhaps they assume that they have already taught their children all of the important lessons of life, when in fact it was the older ones, not the younger ones, that received that focused instruction.

God has, in His infinite wisdom, given us everything we need that pertains to life and Godliness (2 Peter 1:3). Our Lord was good to include in His Word this nugget of wisdom for us to discover. We need to come back to the fundamental principles of life at least once every seven years. As each season of life develops, we find that the unchanging truth of God's Word confronts us in a new and unexpected way. This is a great concept for us as parents, or for those in teaching ministry to the Church, to grasp. We need periodic review, and the younger generation needs to hear some truths for the first time.

CHAPTER

# 4

# THE FATHER'S ROLE

*"And, ye fathers, provoke not your children to wrath: but bring them up in the nurture and admonition of the Lord."* (Ephesians 6:4)

WHY ARE MEN OFTEN SO FAR off the mark when it comes to being leaders in discipling their children? What is the role of the father in the discipleship process?

**Finding Our Place**

I think it is significant that the first thirty chapters of the book of Proverbs are from a father instructing his son on all areas of life. The last chapter, thirty-one, is from a mother instructing her son about how to find a virtuous wife. That should tell us something about the weight that the Scriptures place on fathers' discipling their children.

While there are exceptions to most rules, it is generally true that most men are not detail oriented. Men tend to be good at seeing the big picture. I think men should stay within their strengths when it comes to leading the family. My wife, for example, is quite good at taking big ideas and breaking them down into smaller portions so they can be more easily managed. I'm not good at micro-managing, but I'm good at macro-managing. Between the two of us, we make a great team.

A good father should always be able to identify the main goal in why he is discipling his children and be ready when needed to remind his wife of that chief goal. If you can't readily identify the purpose for your existence, you will never be able to identify the purpose for the training and education of your children.

## The Big Picture

Imagine a pie. Pick your favorite kind. Apple is mine. There are few things in life as sublime as apple pie *a la mode*. Gotta love it! Anyway, slice it into a number of pieces that represent your life. One is your employment/finances, one is your family, one is your church duties, one is your entertainment/recreation choices, one is education, etc. Now, if you are living a consistent life, each individual slice is going to be apple. Unfortunately, most Christians that I know are disconnected in how they view their lives. They say that the entire pie is apple, but they act as though one slice is pumpkin, one is pecan, and so on.

Some have their "spiritual" slice, which includes church, Bible reading, prayer and such, and then their secular life, which usually includes all of the other slices. The goal, of course, is to live a wholly integrated life that isn't disjointed in any way.

Deuteronomy 10:12-13, Ecclesiastes 12:13, Micah 6:8, and Luke 10:27 all define the chief aim and purpose of life. My personal paraphrase of these concepts is this: "I exist to know, love, and serve God, and in doing that I am equipped to love and serve other people."

If that is the supreme end of man (if that is the pie), then every slice of my life must be encapsulated by that mission statement. Why do I work a job? Why do I read books? Why do I buy the things I do? Everything in life has to match up with my life's purpose, or I am being inconsistent.

## Tools for Teaching

The goal then is to learn how to apply the chief purpose(s) of life to every area of our existence. The reason I train my own children is so that they can come to "know, love, and serve God, and by doing so, learn to love and serve other people."

When I ask most Christian parents why they teach their children, they reply, "So they can get a good job." That is like saying the pie is apple, but the education slice is peach. That doesn't make sense. If I ask them why they teach their children math, or science, or language arts, they often reply that they need to know those subjects so that they can get into college. When I ask why they need to go to college, I am usually told that you need to go to college in order to get a good job. So, the chief end of man may be to "glorify God and enjoy Him forever," but the chief purpose of math is to get a good-paying job. This is disconnected. This is *not* a Biblical worldview.

It was for this reason that I wrote my book, *Homeschooling from a Biblical Worldview*, to help parents to be consistent in teaching a truly Biblical philosophy of life through every single academic discipline. The reason I teach my children history, geography, and phonics is that I want them to "know, love, and serve God, and to be equipped to love and serve other people." Teaching the core subjects from a Biblical worldview teaches children to know the God Who created those subjects, and it teaches them to harness the laws of the universe to serve God's purposes in the earth by blessing and serving other people.





**Keeping the Main Things the Main Things**

I believe that fathers must study to show themselves approved unto God, workmen who are not ashamed, rightly dividing the Word of Truth (2 Timothy 2:15). You can only pass on to your children what you yourself possess. Endeavor to develop your own Biblically informed convictions and then learn how to pass those convictions on to your children. To expand your own Biblical worldview, I would encourage you to spend some time studying at my site for apologetics and worldview at www.ChristianWorldview.net

I once read a secular study that said that children were asked what they thought was the most important academic subject. It turned out that it was whatever subject with which their father helped them. The reason given was that children assume that, since Dad is busy, if he is going to take time out of his schedule to help with one subject, *that* must be the most important one.

What this indicates to me is the power of a father's influence. Most of us men work jobs. We are busy. However, we can make a tremendous impact on our children if we are strategic in passing on what is most important.

**What's a Dad to Do?**

There are two duties that the Bible seems to lay nearly exclusively at the feet of fathers: *training and instruction of children* (Proverbs 4:1) and *discipline* (Deuteronomy 8:5, Proverbs 13:1, 24, and 15:5, Ephesians 6:4, Hebrews 12).

For about six years, I served as a volunteer chaplain for a county juvenile center here in Michigan. Of the several hundred incarcerated young men that I have interviewed, only one or two said that they had a good relationship with their father. The overwhelming majority had NO connection with, nor had even met, their biological fathers.

From what I've observed, the overwhelming vast majority of young men who have positive input from their fathers simply don't end up getting arrested and being a menace to society.

The fault of our nation's moral decay can be placed, to a great extent, at the feet of fathers who have not lovingly and mercifully led their children in the ways of the Lord.

**My Approach**

In my home, I take the initiative to make sure that I am leading family worship on a daily basis and that I am staying abreast of my children's spiritual, academic, and emotional progress. I am making sure that I am having "conversations that count" with each of them, drawing them out and probing them with age-appropriate questions to see if they have assimilated what they have been taught and are developing Biblically informed convictions from the information they have received.

I seek to understand my children's personalities, natural skills, learning styles and spiritual condition so that I can lead them in emotionally, spiritually, and academically customized training and discipleship.

While some married couples may choose to handle things differently than my wife and I have, as a homeschooling father, I am usually the one taking the lead in selecting the curriculum that our children use. Part of the reason is that I am more plugged in to what is available or new on the market than my wife (because of my job), but it is also because I really feel that I need to take responsibility as the father to research and know what curriculum approach will work best with each child at each age level. I don't feel that I can just dump that on my wife. I believe it is my job to at least be an equal partner in overseeing the general academic scope and sequence of my children's education.

For us, the curriculum is a means to help us lead our children to know, love, and serve Jesus. The academic subjects are tools in our hands to help them understand the world that God created and to know how to use and capture its principles and laws to serve others in the name of Christ. We use work, service, academic studies, chores, vacation, recreation, entertainment—they all serve together to help us fulfill our mandate as Christian parents.

If this sounds like it might take a lot of time and effort—it does. That's the point! Deuteronomy 6 is a 24/7 year-round endeavor. It's *supposed* to take a lot of time. Where do you find the time? Cut out all of the worthless stuff you are doing that doesn't include your wife and children. For me, that means no golf game, no sports, no fishing, no watching TV after work, no newspaper, etc. If that sounds like legalism, it isn't. It's just realizing I only have a certain amount of hours in each day and a certain amount of years with my children before they are gone.

**On the Airplane**

On a recent road trip I was seated next to a man who makes a living in secular higher education. I asked him about his family, and he told me that he had a twelve-year-old daughter.

"That sounds like quite a transitional age," I mused. "I've noticed that a lot of fathers kind of lose connection with their daughters at that age as they are becoming more independent and involved in activities with peers. In what ways are you being intentional about staying connected with your daughter?"

The silence was awkward. After a moment or two he stammered, "Well, it's hard—I mean, I work a lot of hours, and it just doesn't seem like there is much time left for anything else." He quickly turned and gazed out the window.

I tried to reconnect with him before he shut me out. "The company I work for recently published a book on father/daughter relationships. The author of that book, who is a father of three daughters, has suggested that one way he has been able to stay connected is by having an occasional lunch date with his daughter. It seems to me that it doesn't take too much effort to go to a burger joint and chat for a half an hour a couple of times a month. If your daughter wants to talk, she knows she can. If she wants to just be quiet, that's okay, too. Think of some questions that you could ask to try to draw her out. Ask her how things are going at school, what's going on with her friends, etc. Just let her know that you are there for her and if she needs you, you are available."

We were interrupted by an announcement by the pilot, and it was five minutes before he said anything else. "You know," he finally offered, "you've really got me thinking. I'm going to schedule my first lunch date with my daughter as soon as I get home from this trip."

### The Eternal Perspective

While I am thankful that he is finally thinking just a bit about his relationship with his daughter, I am amazed at how totally ignorant some fathers are. I mean, how in the world can you have a twelve-year-old daughter and not be thinking seriously about how important your guidance and direction are to her life?

Far more than just a mere conversation over a burger and fries, we need to be looking for every opportunity to strategically and systematically equip our children to think and live Biblically. This means that you as the father must be engaged, involved, and leading the way. Your wife isn't supposed to raise and train your children—you are. She is your helpmeet, not the other way around.

When I stand before God, He will hold ME accountable for the spiritual training of my children. I can't hide behind my wife and say, as Adam tried, "This woman you gave me—*she* didn't know what she was doing!" No, I am responsible. The buck stops with me. I am thankful that my wife is a wonderful helpmeet and that she implements well the spiritual blueprints that I am providing for our family, but her role is to come alongside and support the vision that I have received from the Lord and His Word. It's time for us men to grow up and take responsibility for our own families. There is absolutely no valid excuse to do otherwise.

### Exhort, Comfort, and Charge

*"As ye know how we exhorted and comforted and charged every one of you, as a father doth his children"* (1 Thessalonians 2:11, KJV).

I read this verse one day, and it really stood out to me. The Apostle Paul is speaking to the church in Thessalonica, but he gives a description of the role of a good father. It is assumed or presupposed that a faithful father will be doing the following three things with his children.

#### *Exhorting*

The Greek word for "exhorted" is *parakeleo*, which means "to call near," "to invite," "to implore," "to entreat," or "to pray." This word is used most often in the New Testament when someone is beseeching or seeking someone else to follow him or join him. There is almost a desperate cry that is implied in some cases, as someone realizes the importance of having another join him in his journey or struggle.

This is certainly the posture of a father as he says, *"Now therefore, my son, obey my voice according to that which I command thee"* (Gen. 27:8,

KJV), or *"Hear thou, my son, and be wise, and guide thine heart in the way"* (Proverbs 23:19, KJV), or "*My son, give me thine heart, and let thine eyes observe my ways"* (Proverbs 23:26, KJV). A good father is imploring his children to follow him as he follows Christ. This father has a vision. He knows where he is going, and he provides an invitation for his children to join him on the mission.

When I think of this word, Deuteronomy 6 and 11 come to my mind. A father leads his children when they rise in the morning, as they walk by the way during the day, and when they lie down at night.

*Comforting*

The Greek word for "comforted" is *paramutheomai*, which means "to relate near," "to encourage," and "to console." Not only does the father call and invite his children to come to him and follow him, but he draws them in and holds them close. He comforts them and calms their fears. He provides a safe place for them. They know that they are loved and accepted by their father. They understand that nothing can harm them when they are in his arms. They delight in the safety and security that he provides. This is not the picture of the stern and aloof father, emotionally distancing himself from his children, but rather an intimate picture of a father drawing near to his children, being a shelter for them from the ravages of the cruel world.

*Imploring*

The Greek word for "imploring" is *mastigoo*, which means "to discipline." The main usage for this word in the New Testament is to warn someone sternly. It is essential to note the order of the usage of this word in the verse. The idea of discipline or correction or rebuke comes ONLY after the ideas of exhorting and comforting have been well-established. A child cannot properly receive the discipline of a father who has not laid the right foundation of drawing a child near and being a safe shelter. There is a need for a father to provide rules, guidelines, and boundaries for his children, but this must always be done in the context of a loving and caring relationship. As author Josh McDowell puts it, "Rules without relationship breeds rejection."

Hebrews 12:7 assumes that it is the father's role to discipline his children. The Scriptures are clear that a child left to himself will end up in trouble. *"The rod and reproof give wisdom: but a child left to himself bringeth his mother to shame"* (Proverbs 29:15, KJV). There are many examples of fathers whose sons were wayward because of their lack of leadership: Aaron, Eli, Samuel, David, Solomon, etc. A father must not merely be his child's pal. He must provide gentle and strong leadership.

Our Heavenly Father is our model in all of these areas. He demonstrates each of these traits in His relationship with us. Many fathers have not had good examples or models of this kind of balanced fatherhood. Some fathers did not provide any leadership or vision for their children. Some were not affectionate and affirming. Some did not provide discipline or are too harsh or abusive in their application of discipline. This lack of example makes it hard for men to lead in areas in which they have not been led.

We all need to start somewhere, and if you haven't been led by a good role model in these areas, ask God to help you become the man you need to be so that YOUR children will have an example to follow. *"The living, the living, he shall praise thee, as I do this day: the father to the children shall make known thy truth"* (Isaiah 38:19, KJV).

CHAPTER

# 5

# CHILD TRAINING

*"Train up a child in the way he should go: and when he is old, he will not depart from it."*

(Proverbs 22:6)

**Are You Normal?**

A young child's worldview is very complicated. While a child is born with inclinations, he is not born with understanding. To know and comprehend something, you must first have some experience with which to compare and evaluate. An infant has no idea what is normal in the world. For instance, if we were driving down the road and we noticed a neon pink cow grazing in a pasture, we would certainly stop our car and take a photo. Cows are not supposed to be pink! When a one-year-old sees the same cow, he doesn't know that he should be amused. From his limited base of experience, he reasons that perhaps most cows are pink. The scene is not odd to him.

What a sacred trust we have as parents! Our holy responsibility is to teach our child, from his first breath, what is normal and what is right or correct. Heaven help us if we should ever give our child a wrong impression.

**Is Normal Just A Setting On The Dryer?**

In our age of relativism it seems too absolutist to insist that there can be such a standard as "normal." "After all," the skeptic may muse, "what is normal for you, may not be normal for me." The word "normal" comes from the Latin, "normalis" which means, "According to a square or rule." (Webster's 1828) Anyone who has ever tried to build a house knows that you can't do it unless you adhere to absolute principles. You must have some universal standard of measure. Plumb, square and level must mean the same things to everyone on the work crew. If you don't all use the same rules of building, you will end up with disaster.

So it is in our day of pop-culture parenting. Many children today grow up being planted in soil that is abnormal (irregular, deformed). Some parents have a crooked worldview and have twisted ideas of what it means to raise children. Many received their notions from the postmodern smorgasbord of poppsychology parenting magazines, daytime talk shows, self-proclaimed family experts or maybe just from bad experiences they have carried over from their own childhood. Whether they are too loose in their parenting approach (which is most common) or too tight, they are abnormal in their approach to raising their children, and their children suffer because of it. The beliefs and actions of most parents are totally arbitrary, unpredictable and driven by mood swings rather than a Biblical theology of parenthood.

There is a difference between what is common and what is normal. Normal is defined by the nature of God and is explained through His Word. Common is how the majority of people in a certain society choose to live. The majority is often wrong and dysfunctional. Look at how many Germans supported Adolph Hitler! We desire to be normal, but not common.

**Who Wears The Pants In The Family?**

The Bible teaches that children do not belong to parents, at least not ultimately. Some believe that, "It takes a village to raise a family." They feel that parental rights do not exist, and everyone is responsible for everyone else's children. People with the "village" mentality would agree with the statement that children do not belong to their parents, but their view may lead them to meddle in the lives of others and impose themselves in situations where their involvement is neither desired nor helpful. The Bible, however, teaches something very different from this vogue concept of the communal ownership of children. *"Lo, children are an heritage of the Lord: and the fruit of the womb is His reward"* (Psalm 127:3, KJV). In Ezekiel 16:20-21, God emphatically declares ownership of the offspring of His people. He proclaims that these children were born "to Him." God, in His infinite wisdom and mercy, has chosen some of us to be stewards and caretakers of His children.

For those of you who have ever baby-sat someone else's children, you understand that there are many differing values and standards people implement in raising their children. As a short-term custodian of someone else's children, a wise caretaker will seek to understand the wishes of the absent parents so that their values are upheld. Hopefully they have provided you, before their departure, with a fairly exhaustive list of what is acceptable, and what isn't.

So it is with the children that God has entrusted to our care and oversight. We must seek out the instructions the Lord left for us to follow. We cannot care for these children, born of our flesh, with the strength of our flesh. We must learn to parent through the empowerment and wisdom of God's spirit.





**Inappropriate Correction**

The mistreatment of children by their parents is one of the most reprehensible ideas of which we can conceive. There is, as Karl Marx mockingly said, "The most hallowed of relations" between a parent and child. There is a natural bond that is divinely infused between an excited new parent and the helpless child he or she holds. Yet, in spite of this natural and normal connection of heart and soul, there are those who, for whatever reason, neglect that holy trust and wound the body and emotions of the child within their care.

Appropriate discipline of a child is normal. The authority of the parent is normal. C.S. Lewis in Mere Christianity says, "Badness is only spoiled goodness. You must first have the idea of (normality) before you can talk of its being perverted; and you can see which the perversion is because you can explain the perverted from the normal, and cannot explain the normal from the perverted." Lewis also adds, "Evil is a parasite, not an original thing."

Satan cannot create. He can only pervert. Everything that is holy and right in a relationship between a parent and child is defined by God, and purposefully undermined, attacked and mangled by Satan.

**The Heart Is Deceitful and Desperately Wicked**

All of us would like to think we are exempt from committing sinful acts simply because we are "good" people. God's Word is emphatic that no one is naturally good.

*"The heart is deceitful above all things, and desperately wicked: who can know it?"* (Jeremiah 17:9, KJV).

*"Surely I was sinful from birth, sinful from the time my mother conceived me"* (Psalm 51:5, NIV).

*"And Jesus said to him, 'Why do you call Me good? No one is good except God alone'"* (Mark 10:18, NASB).

We have to come to grips with the fact that any of us can fail and commit sin against another person. The more convinced we are of our own moral goodness, the more prone we are to fall. *"Wherefore let him that thinketh he standeth take heed lest he fall"*(1 Corinthians 10:12, KJV).

*"When pride cometh, then cometh shame: but with the lowly is wisdom"* (Proverbs 11:2, KJV).

While we can't know all of the particulars of each individual situation, there are general patterns or root causes that contribute to sinning as parents.

**Selfishness**

We live in a society that promotes self-gratification. As opposed to the Scriptural mandate to deny ourselves (doesn't that concept sound outdated!), we are told that we deserve to do something for ourselves. Men are told that they have a right to their free-time and should have space for their personal interests. Children, by nature of their vulnerability, tend to encroach on a father's desire to unwind and kick back after the hectic pace of a stressful workweek. Children need their fathers. Children have legitimate needs that they are unable to meet by themselves. There becomes a competition between the perceived needs of the father and the pressing needs of the child or children. Someone will have to be denied. It is a rare father who will deny himself to care for the needs of the children entrusted to him.

Society teaches mothers that their only value is found in being a career woman, and their identity must be proven outside the home. They are taught that if they truly love their children they will place them in day-care and let the professionals handle the tough job of child-rearing. Some women even convince themselves that they are sacrificing for the good of the child. In reality, however, it is not normal for a mother to abandon the care of her own offspring to another person, no matter how noble it may appear. The notion that she "owes it to herself," to get a job and have her "own life," is fundamentally no different than the worldview that claims she has a "right" to abort her own child. It is a total violation of the natural order. I'm not addressing the issue of women working outside the home as much as I am the idea that the "life of the mother" is somehow intrinsically more valuable than the life of the child. A normal mother will do everything in her power (even giving up her own physical life) to ensure that the life of the child is preserved. We cannot call ourselves Christians if we refuse to deny ourselves and lay down our lives.

**Anger**

Volumes have been written on the subject of anger. There are many causes for anger, but regardless of why a parent is angry, the child will undoubtedly take the brunt of the parent's heat. Many Christian parents try to hide their ungodly attitudes and fleshly responses under the religious garb of "righteous indignation." The Bible says, *"The wrath of man worketh not the righteousness of God"* (James 1:20, KJV). If you want to bring about the righteousness of God in your children, you will not be successful in accomplishing it through the means of the wrath of man.

We all know Proverbs 22:15, *"Foolishness is bound in the heart of a child; but the rod of correction shall drive it far from him."* Few of us know this verse before it: Proverbs 22:8, *"He that soweth iniquity shall reap vanity: and the rod of his anger shall fail"* (KJV). There is nothing righteous about a parent simply being ticked off and taking it out on a child. The problem is the anger with which parents respond towards their children. Anger is a destroyer.

Obviously when a child does something wrong or destructive, a parent should express his or her displeasure. I'm not suggesting that we should approve of everything our children do. I'm not insinuating that we should pretend to be happy all of the time, even when we are deeply troubled or grieved at the behavior of our children. But I am saying it is not our place to vent our wrath on our children, making them take the brunt of our frustration. A parent who is not self-disciplined cannot properly discipline his or her own children.

Taking your anger out on your child is never excusable. Those who piously refuse to obey the Scriptural mandate to discipline a disobedient child in a loving manner with a rod of correction, are still sinning against their child if they verbally berate them or pour out their anger against them. Hurtful words can be very emotionally damaging to a child.

A child should have a healthy respect of a parent and should expect that defiance and disobedience with be met with correction and discipline. There should be no doubt in the child's mind that their parents' instructions must be obeyed. What a tragedy, however, for a child to cower in fear, quaking in terror because of the unpredictable rage and fury of an uncontrolled parental temper-tantrum. Children should long to be with their parents, and they should not feel relieved when the parent is gone. Children who experience loving, Godly, Biblical discipline love and respect their parents, and want to be around them. A child who flinches at an unexpected motion of a parent is often indicating that they are not being disciplined in a Biblical manner.

**A Loss of Shame**

Selfishness leads to a justification of anger, which leads in turn to a searing of the conscience. Once our hearts are no longer tender to the correcting and rebuking word of truth, we become desensitized and hardened to sin. We justify our harmful actions against others by telling ourselves that our actions are not what they appear to be. I have known abusers and alcoholics who insist that they don't have a problem. They have convinced themselves that their actions are somehow less than pathetic, they are still in control and everything is fine.

In his book, Deliver Us From Evil, Ravi Zacharias explains, "The unbearable reality of secularism's consequential loss of shame is that the ones we victimize by evil can even be the ones we claim to love.... This is the crime we end up witnessing when family members kill their own offspring.... To remove shame is to perpetuate evil even towards the ones we love. The catalog of crimes between families ... is one of the most painful and most incomprehensible. The evils we foist upon children at the hands of responsible adults are not crimes born of hate. They are passions unleashed and justified by a conscience bereft of shame or remorse. Any conversation with a police officer who investigates criminality within families reveals horror stories that stun the mind. Almost every police officer I have met has said to me that if we were to know even a fraction of all that goes on in homes behind closed doors the knowledge would be heartbreaking. Shame is meant to protect the very ones we love. But our culture has killed it. With the Name of God now unhallowed and His Kingdom not welcome does it make any sense to cry, 'Deliver us from evil'?"

**Failures**

Improper discipline runs on a continuum that stretches from the dysfunctional to the truly evil. A parent who "blows a fuse" ranting and raving, storming around the house, taunting, provoking, intimidating, verbally berating and belittling, throwing things, grabbing their child by the arm and yanking them around, shaking them, pulling their hair, slapping them, pushing them, kicking them, purposefully depriving them of needed food, sleep or basic clothing, throwing them around in anger, or randomly hitting them with sticks or other objects, is totally inappropriate in her actions toward her children.

Mistreatment of children can take on extreme forms that boggle the mind in the depths of their evil. We obviously can't list every possible form of mistreatment, but suffice it to say that anything that surpasses the hideous sins we have already described, including any form of sexual abuse, are an abomination that cannot be justified in any way.

*"And, ye fathers, provoke not your children to wrath: but bring them up in the nurture and admonition of the Lord"* (Eph. 6:4, KJV).





**Can You Change Bad Patterns?**

If you realize that you are guilty of mistreating your child (especially if it is a chronic pattern), you need to repent, immediately stop your inappropriate behavior and seek help. You need to learn how to Biblically discipline your child, and that will likely take seeking out counsel from those who are mature followers of Christ. You need to repent to your children for your anger, your selfishness and your failure to use your position of leadership responsibly. Humble yourself before your children and request their forgiveness. Commit before them that by God's grace you want to be a faithful, normal parent. Explain to them what you have done that is inappropriate, and explain to them how things will change (so they will know what to expect). Learn to be predictable and consistent in training your children. Children do not thrive on chaos and confusion.

If you have a problem with anger, God may choose not to deliver you overnight, but you must stop your inappropriate behavior immediately. You need to learn, through God's Word and the counsel of mature Christians who can keep you accountable, how to overcome anger so it doesn't control you anymore.

**Appropriate Correction**

When a child is disobedient, rebellious or defiant, a wise and normal parent will share with them what they have done that is wrong, and will be faithful to apply an already previously explained and age-appropriate consequence or correction.

A parent who consistently administers Biblical discipline to her child from a young age will not have to worry about turning their relationship with her child into a physical or emotional wrestling match. The child will soon learn to receive correction without a struggle.

A parent should never be out of control, yelling or speaking to a child with clenched teeth or bitter words. After following through with appropriate discipline, the normal parent will comfort their disciplined child, holding them close, praying with them, helping them to ask God for forgiveness for their sin, expressing their love once again, and assuring them of their restored place of fellowship within the family.

A child should never feel that their parent hates them, is taking out their anger through discipline or just wants to get even in some way. Discipline is always and only for the good of the child. It is a mercy to our children when it is done right.

**Be the Dad**

It was a great revelation to me some years ago when I realized in my Bible study that every single passage in the Bible that speaks about discipline is directed to fathers, and never to mothers. I think that is significant. Mothers end up doing the vast majority of all child discipline and they often feel burned out and frustrated with the lack of results. I know that in our own family, we gained some wonderful results once I took over my place of leadership on this issue.

**The Discipline Chart**

I have learned that every single time there is a problem with one of our children disrespecting their mother, or having a hardened heart, it is *always* my fault. My wife is a great mom, and does a fabulous job, so when things aren't working, it's because I'm not leading. I'm not saying this is true for every family, but it is for ours, at least so far. It is almost always that I have become too busy in my own work responsibilities that I am not as engaged in the Full-Time Parenting process as I need to be.

When our oldest children were about seven, six, four and two, my wife lamented to me that she was simply not getting anything done because the children were disobeying her all day. She said, "If I disciplined these children, or fussed at them, for every time they disobeyed me, ignored my words, or defied me, I'd do nothing else!"

I knew I needed wisdom. So I prayed about it. The next day, I created, "The Discipline Chart." Now, before you follow this method, I'm not saying this is what every parent should do. This is just what we did, because I felt the Lord was leading me to do it.

The Discipline Chart had three boxes. Suppose my wife told our six-year-old to sweep the kitchen floor (one of her chores) and she instead went off to play Legos with her brother. My wife would march her over to the refrigerator door, put a pen in her hand, and my daughter would place an "X" in the first box. The first two boxes represented a predictable loss of a privilege that they enjoyed. So the first box might be a loss of dessert after dinner that night. My wife would write the specific disobedience over the box so I could discuss it with my daughter when I returned from work.

The next box might be that she would not get to listen to a story CD that night at bedtime. I think it is important to have the child check the box themselves because it is their way of taking responsibility for what they did. They need to check that box with their own hand.

The third box, though, was altogether different. If I came home and found *three* boxes checked, that means that I would give that child an age appropriate consequence.

For the first week, every child maxed out the chart every day. We only did this with the older three because the two-year-old needed immediate correction if he did something bad. His little mind was not developed enough to remember something he had done ten minutes ago, let alone six hours before. Our four-year-old was old enough to remember his actions from earlier in the day and was mentally mature enough to explain to me what he had done and why it was wrong, so he was included.

The deal was that my wife wasn't to discipline at all during the day, unless there was an urgent need. She wasn't to argue with the children, raise her voice, fuss at them, threaten them with loss of privileges, etc. As soon as a child disobeyed, they went immediately to the refrigerator and made an "X." It was kind of a "three strikes and you're out" method in that every infraction after the third box would be included in the conversation we had when I got home and disciplined them.

As I said, we did this every day for a week. I would discipline them, and they didn't like it. My wife's life was already getting better because she had stopped stressing. The weight was no longer on her shoulders, but rather on mine, where it belonged. Discipline is Dad's job. I'm not saying that a mother should not be *allowed* to discipline her children, by no means. I'm just saying that she is Dad's helpmeet, not the other way around.

After one week, *none* of my children would go past two marks on the chart. For the next month, they pretty regularly would get two right off the bat, but then they would dig in their heels and absolutely refuse to allow themselves that third disobedience or defiance. I was amazed. Now granted, if that was how life was going to go for six months or six years, I was committed to it for the long-haul. I was just surprised how relatively quickly things turned around.

My wife was so much more productive and our home was so much more peaceful. I was being a Full-Time Parent. I had been doing what I could before that, but it was realizing that discipline wasn't my wife's job that made me get involved. I thought that because I was at work for long hours of the day, and didn't want to be a big ogre at night when I came home, that I simply couldn't be the lead disciplinarian. I was wrong.

Eventually, the older children had fewer and fewer marks on the chart overall. I believe the change was *not* due to the fact that the discipline was any different than that administered by my wife, or that my children were intimidated by me. Neither was true. The deal was that neither I, nor my children, enjoyed spending our precious time together that way. They didn't want Dad to be unhappy with them. They didn't want to have to tell Dad all the bad things they did that day. They didn't want to have Dad, who they loved and wanted to do fun things with, to spend his precious time disciplining them. It was a relationship issue.

Children want attention. They'll settle for negative attention if that is all they can get, but they respond much more positively to positive attention. They thrived on my coming home and making a big fuss about how happy I was that I didn't need to discipline them. They beamed when I told them how pleased I was that they were learning to be a helper to their mother.

Parents who don't discipline their children often become very frustrated because they have no viable means of restraining their child or making their child obey them. These parents usually live at a very high stress level (as do parents who discipline, but don't do it in a right way). Failure to discipline a child almost always results in a child that no one likes and virtually no one wants to be around.

Discipline is essential because God requires it of you but it must be applied with prayer and wisdom. It is only when you are in alignment with His Spirit of love and self-restraint that you will be able to see the proper fruit from its application.



**The Role of the Church**

It only takes a few unbalanced parents, mistreating their children, to bring a huge blight on the body of Christ. Pastors and church leaders need to be proactive in systematically teaching their congregations how to Biblically discipline and train children. Every "churchgoer" should have heard, from the pulpit or in a special class, how to correctly administer child discipline. Parents should know that mistreating their child is a sin, and that there is no excuse for it.



Knowing how much our Lord loves and values children, we must commit ourselves, as parents, to raising children in a completely loving and Biblical manner. We must never abuse the sacred trust our children place in us. We must learn to abandon anger, discipline consistently and only in love, learn Biblical principles for child training, and then we must eventually instruct others so they can do the same.

The church must be a haven where families can learn what God's Word teaches about how to live together in normal relationship with each other.

Jesus truly loves the little children ... all the children of the world. Little ones to Him belong. They are precious in His sight.

**The Role of the Savior**

Parents, our job is simple: teach our children what is "normal." The hard part is that our "norm" is so astounding: perfect holiness and infinite love. Jesus said, *"Be perfect, as your Heavenly Father is perfect"* (Matthew 5:48, KJV).

Read the Gospels from one end to the other, and the good news of the Father comes through time after time: Our Father loves us.

Our Father knows us. Our Father hears our most secret prayers. Our Father welcomes us in—though we are prodigals who spit in His face. Our Father sent His only-begotten Son to pay the debt we had incurred to make us one family forever.

This truth is so important that it is always under attack. Muslims deny it explicitly—"Allah is not begotten, and He does not beget." The ancient religions of the east depersonalize God, while modern Eastern mysticism would make us all "divine." Secularists call all men "brothers" yet deny that God is Father—but with only Darwin dictating the survival of the fittest, godless men are the kind of "brothers" Cain and Abel were.

This truth about the Father is under attack by every cult and "ism," but it's under attack in Christian hearts and homes as well. Fathers, each time we put our own comfort or "rights" ahead of the best interests of our wife and children, we mock the Father-heart of God. When anger or self-pity prompts our words instead love, we disfigure our Heavenly Father's image. And when, God forbid, we cause one of these little ones who believe in Jesus to stumble, we deserve to have a *"millstone hung around our neck to be cast in the depths of the sea"* (Matthew 18:6).

The bad news is that each of us, as parents, has made a mockery of the Heavenly Father. In our pride, anger, selfishness, self-pity, or fear we have set up substitutes for God. If you have ever raised your voice in anger at a child, consider the infinitely holy Father who entrusted that child into your care. If you have ever failed to discipline a child who was going wrong, consider the Father who commanded us to raise them for Him. What answer will we give on that day when the Father asks, "Did you ever—either through action or through inaction—shake this most precious child's most precious faith?"

That is the "norm," the standard by which every parent shall be measured. There is no parent who is innocent of that charge—and many will suffer the eternal consequences for their abuse and neglect of God's perfect law. But though we are all guilty, not all will be cast away. Though every parent falls short of God's high standard and deserves to be treated as a criminal, God treats certain sinful parents as His own children. And He does that because He treated His only-begotten Son like a sinner.

Jesus, unlike every other child who ever grew up on this planet, never sinned. Jesus, unlike every other son of Adam, never needed correction. Parents discipline children for their own good, but that's not why God sent Jesus to the cross. The Heavenly Father *"so loved the world, that He gave*

*His only begotten Son, that whosoever believeth in Him should not perish, but have everlasting life"* (John 3:16).

*"And whosoever shall give to drink unto one of these little ones a cup of cold water only in the name of a disciple, verily I say unto you, he shall in no wise lose his reward"* (Matthew 10:42; KJV).

*"And whoso shall receive one such little child in My Name receiveth Me. But whoso shall offend one of these little ones which believe in Me, it were better for him that a millstone were hanged about his neck, and that he were drowned in the depth of the sea. Woe unto the world because of offences! for it must needs be that offences come; but woe to that man by whom the offence cometh!"* (Matthew 18:5-7; KJV).

*"Take heed that ye despise not one of these little ones; for I say unto you that in Heaven their angels do always behold the face of My Father which is in Heaven"* (Matthew 18:10; KJV)

CHAPTER

# 6

# HELPING THE HYPERACTIVE CHILD

*"Thou shalt love the Lord thy God with all thy heart, and with all thy soul, and with all thy strength, and with all thy mind; and thy neighbour as thyself."* (LUKE 10:27)

"*THAT* CHILD HAS ADHD. He needs to be on Ritalin!" Thankfully my mother wasn't one to take the advice of every supposedly well-meaning onlooker. As a hyperactive child, I can honestly say that I never "suffered" with hyperactivity. In fact, I rather enjoyed it! It was the people around me who suffered.

There was the time I locked myself in the trunk of our car because I just *knew* that no one could *possibly* find me there (which was true!), or the day I pelted our neighbor's new Cadillac with a well-aimed rock as he drove by, or the time I pulled the church fire alarm during call to worship, or the time ... well you get the point! If you have a hyperactive student you know that it can be a real challenge to keep your own sanity and see anything but a prison record in your child's future!

I am living proof that a hyperactive child can live a productive and healthy adult life. Most of my hyperactive and attention-deficit problems simply went away as I became an adult (which is common for many hyperactive people), but I have also had the advantage of implementing some techniques that helped me tremendously.

For some reason, parents with a hyperactive child feel that their child's behavior is unique to humanity, and no one else has ever faced the task of raising an energetic child. On the contrary, high strung kids go back as far as creation. My life stands as evidence that a child can be successfully parented even if they are hyperactive. In fact, the Bible is filled with stories of hyperactive children.

Take David for example. He was so energetic his mother sent him to the fields every day to kill lions and bears. (David was obviously a hands-on learner.) Or can you imagine being Samson's parent and having to explain to your Philistine neighbors why your son was always beating up their children? And, I've always pictured John the Baptist's mom reading parenting books, and concluding that homeschooling was the only alternative for her son. Besides, the school board would insist he wear "normal" clothes, and exchange his unique cuisine for cafeteria lunches!

All joking aside, training an overactive child is no laughing matter. Many parents feel frustrated and wish their children could just be "normal." Don't be discouraged! If handled properly, a hyperactive child can grow up to be a productive member of society; he may even write a book!





**Hyperactivity Isn't All Bad**

The first thing I'd like to emphasize is the fact that God likes to use hyperactive people. God commands us: *"Love the Lord thy God with all thine heart, and with all thy soul, and with all thy mind"* (Deuteronomy 6:5, KJV). God actually commands us to give Him a wholehearted effort. A hyperactive child does everything with gusto! They always make their presence known. The goal of parents is to work with the child's God-given energy, not destroy it.

I think it is important that we differentiate between being energetic and rebellious. An active mind and body are definitely gifts from God. Vitality and excitement should be welcomed and not quenched. However, sometimes the term "hyperactive" can be a professional excuse for rebellion and outright disobedience. A Scriptural term is "*foolishness*." *"Foolishness is bound into the heart of the child"* (Proverbs 22:15a, KJV). In my case, my mother had to determine when I had crossed the line from simply being energetic, to being out of control and unrestrained. Being consistent is the key. A strong-willed child will always test the boundaries to find out what they can get away with, and if a parent is inconsistent with their discipline there will be no restraining that child.

When I was a child, my mother spent every waking moment trying to keep me out of trouble. I always wanted to know, "What would happen if ..." I had an inquisitive mind that ran constantly, and when I was bored (which was most of the time), I would look for ways to entertain myself.

Once I caught my room on fire doing an electronics experiment, which is part of the reason I was banned from those fun-looking "Science lab in your backyard" programs. The very first computer we purchased was a Mac SE (only found in antique stores nowadays) which Mom bought for work. She kept it in her office and emphasized the fact that it was not for entertainment, and was not a toy! Well, she didn't specifically say that I couldn't use it; she only said it wasn't for playing games. After a few minutes of throwing icons in the trash, which I thought was great fun, Mom discovered that two months of work had gone somewhere into the black hole of digital space. (I was only trying to see what would happen!) When I was about four years old, I untuned every stringed instrument in our church 10 minutes before the service. (There was not a joyful noise that day!) Once, I pulled the church fire alarm ... during opening prayer. We had people at the altar, and the pastor didn't even give an invitation.

When I was about ten, I welcomed the new lady next door to the neighborhood, by hitting a baseball through her kitchen window ... during breakfast. I was even hyperactive as a toddler. Mom said when I was eighteen months old, I escaped from my crib, proceeded to change my own diaper *(Note from my mother: ... Which would have been great—had he only remembered to put another one back on!)* left the house, and wandered through the neighborhood during a snowstorm. Our neighbor noticed me and brought me home, giving my mother a lecture about being an irresponsible parent. A few weeks later, I drank lighter fluid and consumed a few bottles of pills. I ruined all mom's hairpins in the electric outlets. Or then there was the time ... well, I think you get the point!

I remember a teacher asking my mother, "Do you know what ADHD (Attention Deficit Hyperactivity Disorder) is?"

Of course, my mother did.

"Well, *your* son has an *extreme* case of ADHD! He ought to see a professional."

I didn't know what ADHD meant, and I supposed that I must have a rare disease that would probably kill me in a matter of days. Later that evening, after I had willed off all my toys, I asked Mom what was wrong with me. I knew she was trying to keep the truth from me, but I could handle it.

"What is ADHD?" I asked, with pathos in my voice that would've brought tears to the hardest heart.

"It means," she answered nonchalantly, "the teacher thought you were misbehaving."

"You mean I'm not going to die!" I exclaimed.

"Not unless you act like that again," she calmly replied, still ignoring my antics.

I was amazed that professionals had gone through all that trouble to invent a secret code for misbehavior, so they could talk about it without children knowing. It reminded me of when my parents used to spell out B-E-D-T-I-M-E because they thought I didn't know what that meant. I may not have known spelling, but I knew that meant it was time to scream, kick and avoid sleep at all costs. The other word I always knew was I-C-E C-R-E-A-M. When ice cream was spelled, that meant only the adults ate it, and the kids got B-E-D-T-I-M-E.



**Learning Beyond Labels**

I learned later that professionals don't use codes; they invent labels with which they can categorize children and stereotype them. Government education has specialized in putting children in educational boxes and making them fit a certain mold. The problem with that environment is that children can't reach their fullest potential if they are constantly being told they are incapable. I'm thankful that I didn't have to grow up with the stigma of being labeled. My mother knew my unique challenges, and was sensitive to them, but she never allowed me to use a label as a crutch. Instead of overcoming my struggles, I probably would have been content to say "I'm dyslexic, I have ADHD, my mind works faster than my motor skills, I stutter, I can't concentrate, I can't learn, I can't read, I'm just stupid."



A wonderful thing about home education is that the true "professionals" (the parents), are constantly observing their children and are available to give the loving support needed to overcome the difficulties.

**Don't Make Excuses for your Child**

It's important that parents don't make excuses for bad behavior. If my parents had said, "Israel has a chemical imbalance, so we can't expect him to obey," I would have been a literal terror. My mother always knew the difference between being active and being unruly. There is never an excuse for dishonor or disobedience. Should children be disciplined every time they get excited? If so, we wouldn't have accomplished much else when I was growing up! There has to be a certain amount of tolerance given to children or else they will become bitter, but children should always know what behavior is appropriate and what isn't.

Most of my years growing up, my mother was the only parent, so all discipline fell to her. She allowed us to have fun, but when she indicated that things needed to calm down, we knew that meant immediately. She wasn't the type of parent who would tell the child three times before expecting a response. If action didn't follow instruction, parental reaction instituted intervention, which would necessitate immediate discipline, followed by profuse confession, admission, and finally restoration. This plan worked quite successfully, and after a while, we began to see a pattern. When Mom speaks, and we ignore her, we get disciplined. When we obey, we don't get disciplined. Soon, people were asking my mother, "How do you get your children to obey you on the first request?" The trick was she convinced us that she wasn't speaking just to hear her lips flap.

I don't want you to get the feeling that my mother was overbearing or severely strict. She wasn't. In fact, other mothers complained that they disciplined their children twice as much as my mother, but didn't have the same results. Because Mom was so consistent, she rarely had to discipline us. She just spoke ... once.

Again, keep in mind that there is a definite difference between rebellion and being lively. Rebellion, if not dealt with, will explode and become uncontrollable in the teen years. Children who have never been expected to obey will not suddenly become polite responsive individuals at adolescence. By refusing to immediately deal with rebellion, parents teach their children to disobey and dishonor them. If rebellion is dealt with at an early age, parents won't need to worry as much about hyperactivity in the teen years.

In my case, I wasn't purposefully obnoxious or unruly; I was just full of energy and had a hard time restraining myself when a thought popped into my head. When I thought something, I did it (or said it). When I was three, for example, our Sunday school teacher asked my class "What do you want to be when you grow up?"

Each child took their turn with standard answers like "I want to be a farmer, or an astronaut, or the President." When my turn came, I innocently stated "I want to be fat and ugly, like Mr. Ross (our church deacon)." Laughter filled the classroom as the teacher tried to control the pandemonium. (I know I didn't have very lofty aspirations, but I answered truthfully. As a somewhat undersized youngster, from my point of view, Mr. Ross was the pinnacle of the evolutionary process.)

Many children probably would have been severely reprimanded for such a remark, but my mom knew that I really liked Mr. Ross and meant no harm in what I said. Instead of disciplining me, she merely worked on helping me improve my social graces.

**Training is for the Child's Good**

Knowing how to respond to hyperactivity is the real key. Learning the balance between knowing when to discipline, when to instruct, and when to just lighten up and laugh is the challenge facing parents of hyperactive children. When I did something outrageous or embarrassing, my mother would have to evaluate my motives. Was I being disobedient, disrespectful, inconsiderate, selfish, etc., or were my intentions pure?

Sometimes, parents care more about their own image than they do about the development of the child. My mother never disciplined me simply because I had embarrassed her (which I did consistently), but she was always concerned for my spiritual well-being.

A good illustration of this would be an evening meal we had when I was four. My parents were concerned with making a good impression on our dinner guests and reminded me that they weren't Christians so we needed to set a good example. The family finally arrived for dinner and we all sat around the table to eat. Their family wasn't used to praying before the meal, but they politely allowed us to thank the Lord for our food. While we were praying I snuck a glance at the man and his wife who were looking at each other rather nervously. After the prayer, there was an awkward moment of silence as no one really knew what to say next. I was frustrated by the fact that no one was talking so, never at a loss of words, I proceeded to get to the heart of the problem. "Mister, you're goin' to Hell—and so is your wife, and so is your kids!" My mom choked and stuffed a biscuit in my mouth, and Dad remembered something he had left on the burner. Their whole family turned a dark shade of purple, and we finished the rest of the meal in virtual silence.

When they left that evening, I nearly cried, realizing the perilous destiny of this family and our complete failure to communicate it to them. Now, some parents would have waited until their guests were safely in the car and out of ear shot, and then proceeded to threaten the devil out of their child. My Mom, however, knew my intentions, and although I had completely embarrassed her, she didn't punish me. (In the overall scheme of things, she didn't punish me for a lot of the things I did because they weren't acts of rebellion or disobedience, they simply indicated that I needed to learn appropriate restraint.)

She would always sit me down and explain a better means of handling the situation. If I ever did repeat a mistake that we had discussed, it showed that I had crossed the line from ignorance to disobedience or apathy. Disobedience and apathy were not acceptable.

The good news is eventually hyperactive children become teenagers, and in most cases, hyperactivity swings to the other extreme. As teens go through puberty, they rarely have enough energy to tie their shoes, and they usually quit swinging from the rafters around this age. After all, God only gives teens enough hormones to eat, sleep, and grow. In fact, for most parents, it is a struggle to get their teenagers to wake up at 11:00 a.m. to do school work or chores. I tried to explain this phenomenon to my mother. "You see, Mom, I only have x amount of strength, and I can either use it to clean my room or grow canoe-sized feet; right now the feet are a priority." To which Mom would respond, "I'm the one who buys the shoes for your canoe-sized feet, and if you want a new pair, you'd better clean your room!"

In all seriousness, as long as hyperactive children are taught to respect and honor their parents, obey when they are instructed, restrict themselves to appropriate behavior, and use their energies in a positive direction; they can be kind, respectful, obedient, and productive individuals. I was about as hyperactive as they come, but I didn't need drugs or psychotherapy; I simply needed proper guidance, training and discipline. As we all know, when you train a child in the way he should go, when he is old, he won't depart from his training.

**"For better or for worse, we are noticed. We are scrutinized and examined from every angle.... What do you do when your family doesn't qualify for the cover of the next Perfect Christian Family magazine?"**

CHAPTER

# 7

## THE PERFECT FAMILY SYNDROME

*"He that covereth his sins shall not prosper: but whoso confesseth and forsaketh them shall have mercy."*
(Proverbs 28:13)

LIVING IN A FISHBOWL isn't as fun as you might suppose. Sure, you get a lot of attention but, sometimes, it isn't the kind you were hoping for. Sometimes, you wish that when you fail, every now and then, no one would see or care.

How do you deal with the pressure of maintaining "perfect family" status all of the time? How do you make sure the inside of the cup matches its exterior? How do you judge when you are making it, and when you're falling short? What do you do when your family doesn't qualify for the cover of the next Perfect Christian Family magazine?

At some time or another, all of us have considered what it must be like to be really famous. I mean, famous to the point where you can't leave your home without being recognized by the masses. It may seem glamorous to some, but the weight of such a lifestyle would soon become crushing. Face it, most of us can't deal with the unwanted attention we receive now!

All of us struggle from time to time with keeping a proper perspective in the midst of curious onlookers. I can't speak for your family, so I'll share a few thoughts from inside my fishbowl. My mother is the founder and editor for the *Home School Digest* magazine. When you grow up in a family that publishes books and national publications, which are committed to upholding Godly standards for families, you can be assured that you will be watched. Every word uttered, or written, is critiqued by thousands.

My wedding to my wife was pretty high-profile, with our wedding story appearing the next week in the *Arizona Republic*, and later in the *Wall Street*

*Journal*. Within weeks of being married, my wife and I were speaking at conferences together, telling the story of how God put us together in marriage. We didn't ask for the media attention; it was just the path the Lord had chosen for us.

I remember once when we had four children under the age of seven, I was speaking at a conference, and we were eating lunch in a large cafeteria area with perhaps a hundred or more other people. My toddler had just finished eating and was starting to walk around our table. At a certain point he got bored and decided to head out for more adventurous territory. He took about two steps, and I called to him to come back to me. He turned around, looked at me, thought for a moment, and then took off running in the opposite direction. I bolted out of my seat, caught up with him, turned him around and knelt down so I could look him in the eyes. Just as I was about to speak to him, I heard a woman's voice over my shoulder saying to her friend, "This is great! Now we can see how a REAL EXPERT handles a situation like this!"

For better or for worse, we are noticed. We are scrutinized and examined from every angle. Not to be presumptuous, but I would wager (just an expression, please don't write) that your family is under inspection as well. Maybe it's on a smaller scale, but it exists just the same. How do you deal with it? We want to strive to reach the standard of perfection God has commanded, but we mustn't live our lives based on the expectations of other people.

**What Is The Standard?**

The biggest struggle in this area is to maintain proper perspective. We must keep in mind what perfection is, how we discover it, and what to do if we fall short. *"As for God, His way is perfect. God is my strength and power, He maketh my way perfect"* (2 Samuel 22:31, 33, KJV). Not only is God Himself the standard of perfection, He is the only source of strength from which we can attain perfection. We constantly keep the face of God before us. We look not to the right or the left, but fully *"unto Jesus, the Author and Perfecter of our faith"* (Hebrews 12:2, NASB).

How do people generally respond to the standard of perfection? In my experience, there are a couple of reactions.

### They Despise Any Standard of Holiness

I've noticed that people tend to reject any absolute which makes a demand on their life. The cost of discipleship requires that we give everything. As Dietrich Bonhoeffer stated in his foundational book, *The Cost of Discipleship,* "When Christ calls a man, He bids him to come and die." We have received no other call than to give up our own life "for the sake of the call."

We often rebel against such a yoke. Autonomous humans want to be their own god. They want to make their own rules. They don't want any external imposition. Allow me to give a few examples.

When I attend Christian conferences, I like to sit in on as many of the other speakers as I can. Sometimes, my workshop schedules prohibit this, but I like to check out the ideas of others. One session I attended featured a woman speaker addressing other parents. After a few minutes, she made the statement, "I'd like us to look at the 'Proverbs 31 woman.'" The lady in front of me leaned over to her friend and said, "I hate that 'Proverbs 31 woman'!" I laughed out loud at such an impromptu statement, but her remark was actually quite telling.

I've heard dozens of people comment on how they hate magazine and book covers graced by "perfect" families: every child smiling, every hair in place, and everyone in matching outfits (which, by the way, are all clean!). One lady told me, "Those images don't reflect where I live. I have rowdy children and peanut butter on the walls." Even if those pictures don't reflect our personal experience, why do we rebel against them and despise them? Is it because we believe the cover family is being hypocritical? Or is it because we fear they may be genuine?

When we do seminars people often approach us with questions about their children. Mothers tell us how their children are failing, then they turn to us and say, "But, you wouldn't know anything about this. Your children are *perfect*!" The people who make these statements don't know us. They wouldn't know if we were "perfect" or not. They just assume because we are on the platform telling people about reaching for a Godly standard, we must be superhuman. We get really dirty looks from some attendees who say, "So, are you always this nice to each other?" There is an obvious disgust, not only of our family, but of anyone who tries to call families up to a higher standard.

From their comments it is clear that it isn't phoniness they dislike, as much as it is legitimacy. If they could prove we were hypocrites, they could excuse their imperfections, and failure, to reach the standard. They'd be happier to find out that we'd just had a big fight on the way to the seminar, than to learn that our public image matches our private life.

Now, granted, our family is not perfect, just as your family is not perfect. We have our fair share of shortcomings, failures, sins, and character flaws. However, we really do try to live out the life of Christ every day in our home.



**They Idolize "Perfect" People**

Then there is the opposite extreme. There are groupies who hang on every word spoken by a Christian leader. I'm convinced if some leaders told people to hang from a tree like a monkey, there are folks who would do it. The tough thing with these folks is that they look to another family as the standard, and ignore God. When the groupie discovers an imperfection or sin in their idol, the faith of the groupie is shattered. They can't function. They can't pray. All they can think is, "If expert So-and-So couldn't make it, how can I?"



**They Say, "I'll Never Be Perfect, So Why Try?"**

I have found this attitude to be prevalent among many popular Christian authors. The whole concept of laughing off moral failure is completely un-Scriptural. We can't have a "stick a geranium in your hat and be sinful" mentality. I heard a popular female author on television say, "People are always saying, 'You need to hear from God.' I don't know where they get this stuff. I haven't heard from God in two years, and it hasn't stopped me! I just put my shoes on every day, the same way I always have."

This kind of flippant abandonment of holiness and Godly standards of living is eating away at Christian homes. Without treading on too much theological ground here, it is faulty logic to say we should abandon our pursuit of holiness as unattainable. ("Nobody's perfect.") Hundreds of thousands of people play golf, knowing they will never hit a hole-in-one on each attempt. So why try? Why not purposely hit the ball in the woods? Why not land it in the pond or sand trap? In every field of life, we strive to be the best we can be. We mustn't fall short in our highest calling. We mustn't sin to enable "grace" to abound. That is nothing more than cheap grace, not the costly grace that our Savior bled and died for.

*"Not as though I have already attained, neither were already perfect; but I follow after, if I may apprehend that for which also I am apprehended of Christ Jesus. Brethren, I count not myself to have apprehended: but this one thing I do, forgetting those things that are behind, and reaching forth unto those things which are before, I press toward the mark for the prize of the high calling of God in Christ Jesus. Let us therefore, as many as be perfect, be thus minded"* (Philippians 3:12-15, KJV).

**How Should We Respond to the Standard?**

As believers, we have an obligation to be faithful to that which we know. The more we discover about the personality and character of God, the more obedient we must be. Scripture tells us we must actively live out our faith. Our actions prove what we really believe.

**Why Must We Strive for Perfection?**

First, because God demands it. *"Be ye therefore perfect, even as your Heavenly father is perfect"* (Matthew 5:48, KJV). (See also Genesis 17:1, Deuteronomy 18:13, 2 Corinthians 13:11, 2 Timothy 3:17, James 1:4.)

Secondly, we have an obligation to walk uprightly, setting an example for believers (1 Timothy 4:12). People need encouragement from others who are also striving for these Heavenly goals. Like it or not, we represent Christ. That was the calling we received. We have a holy obligation to be faithful with whatever platform God has given us. We must never be like modern sports "heroes," who say, "I'm not going to be everyone's mother! I'm no role model." You are an ambassador for Jesus Christ, whether good or bad. We must run to, and embrace, the chance to be an example for others. We mustn't shrink back or hide in fear.

**When We Don't Measure Up**

Recognizing our need to be "salt and light," we can find that it's tough to deal with the reality that we're shining about as bright as a candle in the wind and tasting rather bland. However, we can't abandon our post. Deserters will have no part of God's Kingdom. It's important to remember that (hopefully) we are all growing. Most of us have matured a lot in the last five years. We should see things more clearly, and do things better, than we used to.

That is the work of the Holy Spirit in our lives, conforming us to the image of Jesus. We are in a discipleship process. Being a Full-Time Parent gives you the context where you can see your child's needs. Spending *lots* of time with your child is the pressure cooker which boils carnality to the surface where it is visible and can be dealt with. Expect it. Plan on experiencing failures. The good news is you don't have to stay there. We don't embrace a message of defeat but, rather, one of victory that says, "Sure, you're a mess right now, but you're growing."





We can't let our failures and foibles spoil what God wants to do through us. We need to keep short accounts with God. Keep the slate clean. If we do sin, *"We have an advocate with the father; Jesus Christ the righteous"* (1 John 2:1b, KJV). Confess your sin, repent, and move on. There is too much work to do, and we should not allow our inadequacies or mistakes to keep us ineffective.

Just as we weren't born adults, knowing all things, we have to grow spiritually as well as physically. I believe strongly in making spiritual landmarks as they did in the Old Testament. One of the purposes of these landmarks, besides marking private property, was to supply a long-lasting reminder of something important. It seems whenever God did something remarkable among His people, they built an altar or made a monument. They didn't want to forget. We should do the same thing in our families. No, we shouldn't pile up hundreds of rocks in our backyard! (The neighbors are already worried enough about us!) But, we should make spiritual landmarks whenever God gives us a significant victory in our home. Write it down in a journal. Get up in a meeting or family gathering and testify of some specific instance of God's goodness to your family. Make sure we don't forget. *"But the path of the just is as the shining light, that shineth more and more unto the perfect day"* (Proverbs 4:18, KJV). It's a process—don't give up!

**How Should We Relate to Other Imperfect People?**

The tough thing about getting the victory over a major hang-up is that we may lose compassion for those struggling with the very thing we just escaped. *We* found the answer, and think *they* should receive the same revelation we did. Maybe they will, but it might take some time. It took us a while. We agonized over it for months, maybe years.

We need to learn to give people space when they aren't like us. Give them time. If they need to know something additional, God will show it to them in time. As Philippians 3:15 says, *"And if in anything ye be otherwise minded, God shall reveal even this to you"* (KJV).

We can't be the Holy Spirit for everyone else. We can lead them to living water, but we can't force them to drink. We can share what Christ has done in our lives, but they may not be ready for the change yet. That's okay. As long as they are still actively seeking God, they will find Him (Jeremiah 29:13).

If we need to confront a brother or a sister regarding a shortcoming in his or her life, we should only do it if we are motivated by love. Don't shoot the wounded. They are probably already feeling guilty about missing the mark, and they need encouragement to make the hurdle, not rejection or judgment. We are to speak the truth (as hard as that can be sometimes), but we should do it only in love. We need to see the sinfulness of their hearts in light of the sinfulness of our own hearts. Only the grace of God enables us to walk uprightly. Without grace, none of us could live right.

**Allow Inspection**

Let's take advantage of the evangelistic opportunities the Lord sends our way. Because our family home educates, we stand out in many ways to others. People take notice of us and the way we live. We want them to see that what makes our family close, and why we really do love each other, is not that we homeschool, but because of Jesus Christ and how He has changed our lives.

Don't hide behind closed doors hoping no one will see the real you. If there are character flaws in your family, they need to be dealt with. If you don't allow those things to be exposed, your home will be like a scene from "Something Stinks in Here, Part 2." Be willing to hear the good, and the bad, from your mentors, or those in your church or support group. That is what accountability and discipleship is all about.

Of what benefit is a support group where everyone is acting or pretending? Why not be real? Share each other's hearts. If you're not doing well, don't lie. If your children are not in a good place, spiritually speaking, don't hide the truth. Ask for prayer, and be willing to change if need be. If you have a rebellious teenager, don't cover it up and make excuses. Face it honestly. Only then can you be a true help to them. If someone confronts you about the behavior of one of your children, thank them for caring enough to let you know. Stop living with the guilt of skeletons in the closet. Clean it out! Get rid of it, and start over.

**A Brother Loves at All Times**

We need covenant brothers and sisters who are willing to walk with us on this road of discipleship. I'm not sure where our family would be without Godly people who are willing to love us unconditionally. Sometimes that love motivates them to rebuke us for moral failure. Other times it moves them to embrace us in our tears or to pray for us when we face seasons of doubt.

If you have people like this in your life, thank God, and never take them for granted. If you don't have these faithful friends, try being that for someone else. God will never allow your life to be 100% output without supplying friends to encourage and uplift you.

Remember, the key is to walk together in integrity. *"And we, with unveiled faces all reflect the Lord's glory, are being transformed into his likeness with ever-increasing glory, which comes from the Lord, who is the Spirit"* (2 Corinthians 3:18). Throw away the masks! Allow the transformation to take place. Carnality is like a cancerous growth—the longer you ignore it, the faster it kills you.

Allow yourself to be accessible even to the members of your own household. After all, our goal is family-based discipleship. If your husband, wife, parent, sibling, or child sees a character flaw in your life, repent and change. If someone mentions a problem they have observed with one of your children, don't be defensive or combative. Welcome inspection from your spiritual authorities, church family, small group, etc.

**Set an Example for the Believers**

The Apostle Paul told the Church at least three times to be imitators of himself (see 1 Corinthians 4:16; 11:1; Philippians 3:17). We see this pattern also in 1 Thessalonians 1:6; 1 Timothy 4:12, and Hebrews 6:12, as well as Hebrews 11. It is not wrong for others to look to our behavior as a guideline for holy living. Are we not to be imitators of Christ? Therefore, in our conduct, speech, and all other aspects of our lives, we must uphold God's standard of perfection in absolute purity. We have received no other calling. This is truly the call which we heard from Christ, to give all we are, for all He is. Let us embrace it, and rest in it.

Our world is in need of love. It is also in need of leaders who aren't afraid to stand up and be counted. We can truly represent Christ in this post-Christian culture. As the Body, we need each other more now than we have at any other point in American history. The world needs us. Christ is calling—will we answer?

**"YOU KNOW WHO YOU ARE, TO A GREAT EXTENT, BECAUSE OF YOUR RELATIONSHIPS WITH THOSE OF YOUR SURROUNDING FAMILY. FAMILY CAN SERVE AS A FIXED REFERENCE POINT, LINKING YOU TO GEOGRAPHY AND TO THE PAST IN A WAY THAT NO OTHER FRIENDSHIP OR COMMUNITY CAN."**

CHAPTER

# 8

# FAMILY CULTURE VS POP CULTURE

*"My son, hear the instruction of thy father, and forsake not the law of thy mother."*

(Proverbs 1:8)

Although it is never objectively accurate to say that a certain time period was "the good old days," there are many positive values that our society has lost in the past 150 years. One of the most tragic of these losses was the disintegration of the family culture, and especially multi-generational connections and legacies.

Because many of us have never experienced the benefits of the family culture in our lifetimes, we may not even recognize our collective loss. Imagine with me, if you can, a culture where you are surrounded with people who know and love you. There are parents, uncles and aunts, cousins, grandparents and even on occasion great-grandparents. Living, working, playing and worshiping with these loved-ones create a wonderful sense of security and stability. You know who you are, to a great extent, because of your relationships with those of your surrounding family. Family can serve as a fixed reference point, linking you to geography and to the past in a way that no other friendship or community can.

Allow me to outline some of the paradigm shifts that have occurred in American culture over the past 150 years, bringing about a disconnected and individualist society which has replaced the previous family-centered culture.

## The Breakdown of the Family Culture

I would say that the breakdown of the family culture in America began largely after the Civil War in 1865. Over 620,000 American men died in a war that left virtually every family without a loved one. In the Reconstruction that followed, men often left their homes and began to work in factories, taking advantage of the new breakthroughs of invention and industry. Prior to the Civil War, the majority of Americans was agrarian and rural and worked on family farms or in family-owned businesses.





**The Industrial Revolution**

At the turn of the 20th century, it became clear that the machine was the way of the future. From Eli Whitney's cotton gin, to Henry Ford's automobile, from the steam engine to the success of the Wright Brothers' flying machine, people were finding faster and more efficient ways to do everything, including get around.

Wise families started their own businesses and hired family members to keep their income "in house." Around the turn of the 20th century, many families became famous for developing financial systems that grew the family wealth exponentially. The Rockefellers, Vanderbilts, Studebakers, and later the Kennedys, are all examples of family wealth. Whether you admire or disdain that kind of economic nepotism, you have to admit that they knew the collective potential of the family culture.

For most families, however, mass production and factory labor took at least one parent (usually the father) away from the home and children and into the "workforce."

**Government Education**

In 1840, Horace Mann had established the first State-funded, compulsory, government-controlled school in Massachusetts. This model spread around the country and, before long, not only was the father removed from the home, but the children were as well. Instead of children working alongside their parents, receiving an education through family enterprise (and supplemented with either homeschooling or formal academics in a community-controlled "Common School"), students were now enrolled in "assembly-line" educational factories that utilized the Modernistic principles that were revolutionizing every other industry.

More important than the physical separation that occurred through mandatory governmental education was the emotional distance that was experienced as children embraced the culture of "social education." Friendships through the "peer group" replaced the family as the child's primary, foundational relationship.

**Women's Liberation**

Eventually the 20th century "Feminist Movement" put mothers into the workplace as well, effectively removing the central hub of the family from the home. Mothers were convinced to leave the education of their children to trained and certified "experts." With the additional tax burden placed on families because of State-funded schools, many families felt the need to have two incomes just to make ends meet. There is no way to estimate the effect that the so-called "Women's Liberation" movement has had on the lives of millions of children. Children need both parents (ideally) to be emotionally and socially balanced, but they especially need the daily nurturing of their mothers.

While some point to the positive gains made through "equal rights" movements like Women's Liberation, the "freeing" of women from their families has devastated the family culture. Women's Liberation mainly "freed" women from their children and made them slaves to their jobs. It's not merely a matter of men and women working a job outside of the home; it is a mindset shift from parents being responsible for the care and nurturing of their own offspring, to an expectation that the government is supposed to provide for all of our needs from the cradle to the grave, and we all work to support an overgrown bureaucracy that seeks to do for us what we should be doing for ourselves.

Mass distribution of the birth control pill in 1950 further liberated women from children, encouraging them to limit their family size to one or two children. Day cares began to spring up to allow mothers to place babies who were only a few weeks old into the hands of unknown caretakers. Increasingly, family life was sacrificed on the altar of economic pursuits. This has become the overwhelming trend in most of Europe and Asia as well. Many nations have fallen behind the 2.1 child-birth ration needed to keep a society economically viable and they have slipped into economic depression. There are more senior citizens to care for, and not enough wage earners (or family members who care) to provide for them. The United States has a birth rate of 1.8 children per household and is the only nation in the world that is losing population by birth but gaining by immigration.

**Mass Transportation**

More than any other factor, mass transportation destroyed the extended-family culture. As new economic opportunities beckoned, families uprooted from the old home place and took off across the country. The railroad, and later the automobile and the airplane, gave people a new mobility that changed the landscape of America.

Since the telegraph, and eventually the telephone, allowed families to keep in touch over the miles, many families made the choice to exchange local relationships with their extended families for distance ones. This geographical distance removed economic interdependence, and thereby removed a primary reason for staying connected. Working together for a common goal is great cement to bond relationships.



**The Loss of Folk Culture**

America is a nation of immigrants. Groups of families have come to America from every nation around the globe. They bring with them their own beliefs, cuisine, dress, language, and religions (in other words, their own culture). America has become the great melting pot. The tension these families experience (which is really the same struggle that every newly married couple faces) is how to keep their own unique identities while being absorbed into the greater whole. Many ethnic groups have fought tenaciously to keep their families together in the face of what seems like a relentless and pervasive attempt to strip them of their distinctives. As each generation follows, less and less of the "old ways" are retained as the new generations become absorbed into the larger, homogenized American culture. But what is the new American culture? It is no longer the "folk culture" of each of these unique groups; it is instead an emerging consumer culture of entertainment and merchandising; in other words, a popular culture.

**Mass Media and the Creation of a Mass Culture**

With the advent of radio and eventually television, all Americans, regardless of their geography, had access to the same news and information. Mass media and standardized education helped to shape a general culture. Rather than localized, provincial folk or agrarian cultures, Americans were increasingly adopting the lifestyles of urban and suburban society. But regardless of whether you lived in the country or the city, you were watching the same televisions shows, hearing the same commercials, and using the same textbooks as everyone else in America.

### The Advent of Pop Culture

As corporate marketers learned how to tap the vast potential of various media channels, people were slowly morphed into consumers rather than self-sufficient producers. Mass retail distribution through superstores, which sell everything from groceries to household goods, placed all of these nationally advertised products on shelves within a few miles of nearly every American citizen.

The differences between the previous era of folk culture and the new popular (pop) culture are quite stark. In the folk culture of the mid-19th century, for example, families who enjoyed music would create their own music by playing together on the front porch, many times with homemade instruments. Occasionally they would be joined by their neighbors, who were often extended relatives.

Contrast that with the teenager who now listens privately to his Mp3 player, subtly shutting out the rest of the world around him. Folk culture was all about accountability, community, resourcefulness, and creativity. Pop culture is all about liberation, autonomy, spending aimlessly, and consumerism.

While some may seek to defend pop culture and look for its virtues, it is clear that whenever you exchange one type of culture for another, certain things are gained, and others are lost.

Convenience is perhaps the chief gain of pop culture. You no longer have to work together as a family or a local community to grow, can, and store your annual food supply. You just go to the national superstores down the road and buy your garlic from China and your pineapple from Costa Rica and your coffee from Colombia. This is a tremendous time savings, and can certainly be understood as being a gain in many ways. But there is a great loss in this way of life as well.

We have become far more dependent on impersonal, non-relational industries to supply our every need, and far less on personal relationships, especially of those within our own extended family.

So much of pop culture disconnects us from relationships. We turn on and tune out. Television, the Internet, and much of the entertainment industry are created to make us passive consumers, silently absorbing hours upon hours of often meaningless "information" that is usually an end in and of itself, rather than an equipping means to some greater goal or purpose.

**Multicultural?**

We hear a lot about multiculturalism these days, especially in government schools, but personally I observe very little of it. I think a lot of people, particularly those in political power (regardless of party affiliation), are afraid of a truly multicultural society. A truly multicultural society cannot be easily controlled and manipulated. Therefore mandatory "group think" has been the goal of many top-heavy governments over the past 100 years.

If you don't have distinct differences in cultures within your nation, then you are a monolithic culture, not a true multi-culture. The only way to truly preserve a culture (which is the accumulative sum of the beliefs and values of a people group, externally expressed through their art, music, literature, food, dress, religious practices, etc.), is to maintain an inter-connectedness (which usually includes a certain level of interdependence) and to maintain a mechanism for passing on the shared beliefs, values, and customs of that culture.

Homeschooling is the premiere way for any kind of folk culture to preserve its own unique identity while slowly embracing the universal, enduring values of the larger whole of the country. Regardless of your religion or other cultural values, you cannot expect the children who are born a generation or two after you to embrace your values if they are cut off from their familial roots. I believe the castration of unique family heritages and values is being systematically carried out through standardized, compulsory education, and is reinforced at nearly every point through pop culture's synthesized worldview.

We are all expected to accept the notion that we are merely workers and consumers in the greater society and that we must trust the experts (and those in control of the government) to lead us, teach us, and direct our futures.

**What's the Big Deal?**

To some, none of this is important. If the values of the current popular trends have already become your own, then who cares about all of this cultural distinctiveness and familial identity? Who cares about the Family Culture and being connected to the generations who precede and follow you? Who cares about ensuring mechanisms of restraint, accountability, responsibility, and obligation within the larger family context? Who cares about passing on values from your children to their children and to generations who have not yet been born?

If these values are not important to you, then rest assured that your task is easy. All you need to do is nothing in order to ensure that your children will embrace whatever cultural trends happen to be hip at the moment. If you want your children to grow up to love only themselves, think only of themselves, see no obligation to their parents or grandparents, make all of their major life choices with no regard for how it impacts their extended families, or to be simply users and consumers rather than creative producers and artisans, then your task is very easy indeed. Just do absolutely nothing. Send your children to any local government school, let them grow up with their little brains saturated in television and multimedia, and never, ever encourage them to build, read books, dream, play outside, have discussions with their gray-headed relatives, or to see themselves as part of a family unit. I promise you that you will be successful in raising one more pop-culture deadhead.

### Our Mission, Should We Choose to Accept It

It takes work to pass on family values. It takes work to maintain family relationships. It takes work to think in terms of a multi-generational vision. For me, the work is worth it.

I don't want to merely curse the darkness. We can't turn back the clock and become Amish (although I'm sure I'd enjoy that—about 60% of the time!). Perhaps we can find creative ways to use technology and communication tools to keep us together, rather than splitting us apart.

Maybe we can find ways to live in this 21st century without being absorbed in the narcissism of it all. Perhaps we can keep the positive and enduring values of the generations past, while enjoying the comforts and conveniences of our modern age. The one thing I can assure you of, however, is that strong family bonds and the transmission of the right kinds of values never happen by accident. It takes intentionality, focus, planning, and a lot of hard work. Let's learn from the lessons of the past and seek to shine a light for future generations.

CHAPTER

# 9

# TECHNO PARENTING

*"The thing that hath been, it is that which shall be; and that which is done is that which shall be done: and there is no new thing under the sun."* (ECCLESIASTES 1:9)

WRITING ON TECHNOLOGY is a bit tricky. First of all, whenever you use the term "technology," you immediately date your writing. I mean, if you pick up a magazine talking about how wonderful the new 8-track player is, you immediately know something about the age of the article. (I would go so far as to say that if you even know what an 8-track player is, you may know something of your own age! Just ask your teenagers. They'll explain to you exactly how old you really are!) In case you are wondering how I know about them, I uh ... I uh, saw one in a museum once! Heh, heh.

However, I have concluded that technology and the family must be addressed. We will see more technological changes in the next few decades than entire centuries in history have observed. Scientists (and computer developers in particular) are on the verge of technological breakthroughs we can only barely fathom. Computers and satellites have revolutionized nearly every industry. Political experts, educators, and market specialists all agree that a student growing up in the 21st century without basic computer skills will not be able to compete in the ever-changing global economy.

I hope this study will expand our thinking and cause us to follow more closely the will of our Savior in this matter. The focus of this discussion will deal primarily with the Internet since I believe it is the form of technology that has the greatest implications for families in the future and it is a method of communication that is largely unscrutinized by most of us.

**What Is Good About Technology?**

In my estimation, one of the fundamental purposes of technology should be ultimately to enhance the production of goods and services. We live in what is known as an "information age," and much of the Internet exists to host millions of pages of "content" and "information" for viewers to read and download. One company has spent millions of dollars in national television advertising to promote their site full of "content." Even after seeing the ad, it is hard to determine exactly what it is that they do. They seem to simply sell "content."

Information is a good means, but it is a terrible end. To quote the wisdom of the Apostle Paul in his letter to the Corinthians, "*Knowledge puffs up*" (1 Corinthians 8:1b). If the Internet is to endure as anything other than a virtual escape from reality, or a bastion of hedonistic pleasure and entertainment, it must help us produce better goods and services or live better lives. Information in a vacuum is useless (or destructive); it must help us do something better.

Of course, the truly astute will point out that this very book is information-based and that I am using words to question the endless use of words. Yes, but I trust that the Lord will use the ideas in this book to help you disciple your children or to bring your family closer together. It does serve a utilitarian purpose. Any good form of technology will enhance and improve what God has called us to do with our lives.

As a means of communication, the Internet can and should be used for evangelism, building up and equipping the saints for ministry, and providing businesses with more effective means of producing or marketing their goods and services. I'm not implying that everyone needs to use the Internet, but those who do should use it wisely for the Lord. "*And whatever you do in word or deed, do all in the name of the Lord Jesus, giving thanks to God the Father through Him*" (Colossians 3:17, NIV).

**Amusing Ourselves to Death**

Much of technology exists as a vehicle for entertainment. Computers and television are largely used by American children to play games or to enjoy entertaining shows. I certainly have nothing against relaxing and taking a break (presupposing, of course, that we are living purposeful lives where rest is peripheral and serving is central). We need to have something to rest *from*, after all. (How do you rest from being lazy?)

Yet, it does bother me that today's youth are, as Neil Postman (author of *Technopoly*) puts it, "amusing themselves to death." Being entertained is not something that many American teenagers "do" so much as who they "are." It seems that popular culture and media expect teens to simply exist as containers who are to be filled with the expensive content (no matter how useless) of whatever music or programming they wish to propagate. It is almost as though entertainment is a moral good and teens have an obligation to see that it survives. Today's teenagers (now referred to by sociologists as the "Net Generation") are called to keep the e-industry alive, much the same way that they should donate to save the whales (if they were ever to have enough money left over from their latest electronic game purchases).

Technology has an addictive nature. It is very easy to become hooked on it, almost like a narcotic. Entertainment is often used for the same reasons that most people use drugs or any addictive substance: to pursue pleasure and to relieve pain.

Many people entertain themselves because they want to feel good and enjoy themselves or because they have a deep emotional void that they are trying to fill. They want to abandon themselves in a "virtual reality" and forget about the harshness of the life they are entrapped in. People who are entertained for these reasons are liable to escape not only from reality, but from reason as well.





**Technology as a Tool**

Biblically speaking, neither technology nor entertainment is mandatory moral imperatives, and, in my view, they are worthless unless they help us do important things better or more efficiently. In regard to having children use technology in their education, I would strongly admonish you to consider the following: "What call has God placed on your child's life, and what forms of technology will help your child achieve success in what God has called him to do?"

For example, if you believe that the Lord is drawing your child into a career as a chemist, by all means utilize the appropriate technology available in that field. Microscopes, computer research, testing equipment, etc., will all be a part of fulfilling God's purpose in your young child's life. However, if he is going to be an organic gardener, he will probably benefit more from books, mentoring, and getting his hands dirty than by buying expensive computer equipment. For those of you who do organic gardening and surf the web as well, if you can use technology to help you become a better gardener, then I propose that you do so (for the glory of God). I just question how much of what we do with computers and electronic gadgets makes us more efficient and effective and how much of it slows us down and hinders our usefulness for God's Kingdom.

To illustrate the point, I'm going to resort to the realm of the ridiculous for a moment. Let's say that you have a construction worker who buys a new framing hammer and is totally infatuated with it. While his co-workers are busy putting up a house, he sits at the job site admiring his new "waffle head." He has made the mistake of viewing his hammer as the chief end, as opposed to it being a tool that enables him to build the house, which is the ultimate goal.

Many folks view the Internet or television in the same way. They admire the tool and see it as a necessary good, simply because it exists and they like it. The fact is that all media are "educational." We need to make sure we are being educated in beneficial things.

**Striving to Rest**

I know I probably sound extremely utilitarian at this point. Some of you may be thinking, "Doesn't this guy believe in fun?! Are we never to play games or enjoy life?" I believe in rest and renewal, but I think there are some general Scriptural guidelines that apply. We need to be purposeful in our resting. There is a tendency to "vege-out" when we are emotionally or physically wasted, but this can be dangerous. Especially when our body and mind are weak, it is not very wise to indiscriminately give ourselves over to mindless input. It was during one of these "vege-out" sessions that King David gave his heart over to a lustful, illicit relationship with Bathsheba (2 Samuel 11).

The Word instructs us: "*Rest in the LORD, and wait patiently for him*" (Psalm 37:7a, KJV). "*How long will you love vanity and lies? Stand in awe, and sin not; commune with your own heart upon your bed, and be still*" (Psalm 4:2b, 4, KJV). "*Be still, and know that I am God*" (Psalm 46:10, KJV). "*Study to be quiet*" (1 Thessalonians 4:11a, KJV).

In our day and age it is a struggle to rest. Electronic input is not always restful; it is often stressful. If the only way we know to unwind is by turning on the some kind of noise or by watching a screen, I would venture to say that we are addicted to technology. I believe the majority of working Americans today struggle with some sort of attention-deficit problem. There is so much that competes for our notice. Distractions in the form of advertisements and media abound. I believe the enemy of our souls desires for us to be so busy that we have no time to be quiet and still before our Lord. Satan will even settle for "Christian" entertainment if that is what it takes to pull us away from God. You see, it is only in those quiet moments that we say, "*Search me, O God, and know my heart; try me and know my thoughts. And see if there be any wicked way in me, and lead me in the way everlasting*" (Psalm 139:23-24, KJV).

It is hard work to clear our minds of temporal, earthly things and focus on the truly significant. It is a discipline to lay aside the "tyranny of the urgent." As the writer of Hebrews says, "*Let us labor therefore to enter into that rest, lest any man fall under the same example of disbelief*" (Hebrews 4:11, KJV). Our Savior said, "*Come unto Me, all ye that labor and are heavy laden, and I will give you rest. Take My yoke upon you and learn of Me, for I am meek and lowly in heart; and ye shall find rest unto your souls. For My yoke is easy and My burden is light*" (Matthew 11:28-30, KJV).





Even in our rest and relaxation, we are to turn to Jesus. We must not allow anything to pull our eyes away from Him. I'm not suggesting a kind of pietism that removes us from anything that is earthly to embrace only the "spiritual." "*What I mean, brothers, is that the time is short. From now on those who ... buy something [should act] as if it were not theirs to keep; those who use the things of the world, as if not engrossed in them. For this world in its present form is passing away. I would like you to be free from concern*" (1 Corinthians 7:29-32, NIV).

The best way to be free from concern is to use the things of earth for the Kingdom of God. We must not allow them to hinder our pursuit of Him. Even in our rest and relaxation, we should use those times to be renewed and refueled for Kingdom work. Jesus enjoyed times of relaxation with family and friends, but His life was characterized by His focused devotion to the purpose of the Father.

**Content and Form**

There are two important factors that have to be included in this discussion. We need to evaluate the content (information) of technology and also the form (the method of transmission). I find that Christians are much more equipped to evaluate the content of various media than they are to understand potential destructive elements in the form or the means of communication. For example, it is easy to denounce a website that promotes immorality as being unfit for use in the Christian home. However, what about the vehicle that brings that website to you?

As one author says, "Parents are rightfully concerned about the topics of many television shows. However, lost in such discussions is the fact that whether to watch television in many families is too often a foregone conclusion, and what to watch seems to be the only debatable issue."

**The Medium Is the Message**

Are there negative aspects to the forms of technology themselves that we should question? Obviously, we don't want our children playing video or computer games where violence and cruelty are encouraged. But can the process of playing the games themselves be harmful? Michael Medved (author of *Hollywood vs. America*) has said that the problem with television is not only the violence, profanity, and sexual content—it is just too much TV!

For example, there are physical considerations to spending inordinate time before a monitor. Watching TV, playing video games, or typing on a computer can all have harmful side effects to our mind and body. We can develop eye strain, become overweight or develop poor physique from lack of exercise, we might get carpal tunnel syndrome from typing too much, we may develop various stress-related illnesses or headaches, etc. We shouldn't become paranoid, of course, but we should be aware that the content of technology is not the only destructive element. Computers and television can have harmful side effects even if we are only viewing good content.

**The Dark Side of the Net**

Under the heading of harmful "content" I would list the obvious: pornography, violence, new age propaganda, paranormal activity, profanity, and on and on. As the Apostle Paul says, "*the acts of the sinful nature are obvious*" (Galatians 5:19, NIV).

While these things are generally clear to most Christians, there is an insidiousness about "the net" that has a real potential of ensnaring us. They don't call it a "web" for no reason! Let's look at a few of the pitfalls for Christian families using the Internet.

*Unauthorized Relationships*

I have seen families, who I believed were Godly and seeking the Lord, totally shipwrecked by allowing unchecked technology into their homes.

Many will argue that there were obviously already "heart" problems in place and that technology had nothing to do with the spiritual demise of these folks, but I know that just as technology can be a tool for good it can be used by the enemy as a tool of destruction. No, we can't blame the tool exclusively, but it does play a part. Just as a teenager who commits murder after hundreds of hours of listening to music containing violent lyrics cannot blame the songs, it is ludicrous to say that what we input into our lives will never come out. "*For as he thinks in his heart, so is he*" (Proverbs 23:7). You become the sum total of what you fill your life with. As Philip D. Patterson says in his book *Electronic Millstone: Christian Parenting in a Media Age*, "We will eventually reflect what we look at the most. If we spend time in the Word, we will reflect it in our lives. If we spend an inordinate amount of time with the media, we will reflect the world."

I personally know three families who name the Name of Jesus yet who have gone through a divorce after an adulterous relationship developed online. In two of the cases it was the women who "fell in love" with men they met in chat rooms. In the third, a man met another woman hundreds of miles away who he thought fulfilled his dreams, and he left his wife and two children to move across country to be with his new lover. The two women were homeschooling moms with many children, and the man was a fellow with whom I had been in a Bible study.

The Apostle Paul warned of women who get into the habit of going from house to house: "*And not only do they become idlers, but also gossips and busybodies, saying things they ought not. So I counsel the younger [women] to marry, to have children, to manage their homes and to give the enemy no opportunity for slander. Some have in fact already turned away to follow Satan*" (1 Timothy 5:13, NIV). You can go from "house to house" via the Internet without ever leaving home. What may seem like harmless "chatting" online can be the tool the enemy uses to ruin our homes. As C. S. Lewis once said, "There is no neutral ground in the universe. Every inch is claimed by Christ and counter-claimed by satan."

*Unprofitable Relationships*

My wife pointed out to me that not only are unauthorized

relationships a problem on the web, unprofitable ones are as well. As usual, I think she has a good point! Some people chat to others online because they need a support group. That isn't necessarily bad, but sometimes spiritual needs cannot be met by the virtual community.

I remember one situation that arose on an email loop for house churches. One of the fellows on the list was a rather indiscreet chap who loved to argue and didn't demonstrate very many fruits of the Spirit. Finally the group got tired of trying to minister to him and had a virtual "excommunication." They wanted to function as the Church to this guy who needed to be discipled, but all they were able to do was kick him off the list. Some people don't want to be helped, and others simply can't be ministered to because of the limitations of cyberspace.

Regardless of what we may think, virtual friendships are simply not as good as having someone to talk to face to face. An arm around the shoulder, a hand of friendship, and hearing the laughter of someone we love cannot be replaced by "LOL!" (an Internet term for "laugh out loud"). As an aside: One lady who constantly saw people typing "LOL" in their emails assumed the acronym stood for "lots of love." Seeing a good witnessing opportunity, she began ending all of her correspondence with "Jesus died for you, LOL!" It helps to learn the terms if you are going to communicate online! This is another example of how true communication gets lost in the impersonal world of computers.

*Pornography*

While pornography is perhaps the most publicized "dark side" of the net, its potential for harm should not be underestimated. I have often compared the Internet to most public libraries where you can access both good and filth depending on what you go looking for. The difference between the two is that in a library you won't have a pornographic book or magazine leap off of the shelf and suddenly appear before you. Banner ads (ads which scroll across the top of web pages you are viewing), "spam" (unsolicited email), and harmless searches on search engines are all ways that you can be exposed to pornography, like it or not. Many pornographic companies purposefully register religious and educational keywords with search engines to draw in children and religious people. So your child might be doing research online and inadvertently be led to a page that they would have never gone out looking for.

“Sexting” with cell phones is a major problem with teenagers (and many adults). Many teens send each other inappropriate photos or sensual text messages, often without their parents knowing. One family told me that their fifteen-year-old son had nude photos of a girl from his church youth group. She had texted the photos to her boyfriend, who had sent them on to all of his other male friends.

I would strongly encourage Christian families to use porn-blocking software. There are several that cost less than $100 per year. Many offer various levels of parental controls. This will not completely eliminate any access to objectionable sites (there are just too many sites on the net) but in most cases it will vastly reduce the risk of someone stumbling on something destructive on accident.

*Loss of Privacy*

It seems the Internet is one of the most sophisticated information gathering resources in the history of humankind. Companies store all sorts of data that they learn about visitors to their website. For example, if you place an order while shopping at an online store, it is likely that you will be greeted by name the next time you visit their site and given an opportunity to choose from some pre-selected items they think you might be interested in buying, based on your previous purchases. They build a database profile of you as a consumer, and they try to advertise to your specific interests and hobbies.

While that seems harmless enough (albeit somewhat unnerving and annoying), it simply points out how much everyone seems to know about us these days. We get phone calls at our homes from people we have never heard of trying to sell us things we don’t want. How do they get our phone numbers, anyway? We place an order with an online company, which promptly sells our email address to a dozen other companies that “spam” us with offers for everything under the sun. And, of course, there is always the age-old fear of the government spying on us for reasons unbeknownst to us. On the web, it seems that sinister criminals and maniacs who develop viruses for fun are able to maintain anonymity, but the rest of us become victims of our relentless information-gathering society.

As mobile technology has increased, people can use social media applications to inform their social networks of their every move. They are “checked-in” to various businesses, and their every move is cataloged, not only by their friends and relatives, but also by businesses and, in some cases, criminals who stalk them or rob them blind since they know they are not home.

*Wasting Time and Internet Addiction*

The interactive nature of the Internet has an addictive element. It is real easy to plan to go online for 15 minutes and end up spending an hour surfing around looking at various websites. That is how the web is designed. Everything is vying for your attention, trying to get you to click a banner or link to take you to another site that promises an informative news brief, a sale on an item you have been wanting, or the opportunity to win some prize. The world is at your fingertips, and it is hard to discern when you should turn it off.

One homeschooling mom who was a regular on a homeschool chat forum found that she was spending four hours per day chatting with other moms about how to be a better wife and mother! She had become addicted to chatting and was beginning to lie to her husband to explain why she hadn't accomplished anything during the day. She would tell him that she was sick and had to stay in bed to try to recover. Of course, this caused a double anxiety for the husband, who was concerned not only about the dishes and laundry piling up everywhere, but also about his "ailing" wife.

On a plane recently, I was talking with a young man from Dallas, Texas, who maintains a web server for his company. He spends at least 70 hours a week on the computer. He has five computers in his home, and he has to check email every couple of hours or else he begins to panic. He was on his way to visit his mother in Nappanee, Indiana, where he had been raised. (Nappanee is known as a prominent Amish community.) I said, "Well, you will probably be glad to get away from computers for a week, won't you?" "Actually," he laughed, "my mom wants me to work on fixing her computer while I'm there. And, I can check my email and work on our company's server from my mom's high-speed internet line." I asked him if he thought he could go 48 hours without touching a computer. He admitted that he knew he couldn't.

Texting and "tweeting" (a term made popular by the site "Twitter"™) are a huge addiction for many people. One famous Hollywood marriage ended because the husband was so addicted to messaging on his phone that his wife said she couldn't take it anymore and left him!

*Instant Gratification and Attention Deficit*

As if Americans weren't impatient and stressed out enough, along comes the Internet with even greater promises of immediate satisfaction and fulfillment of every desire. Children, who already lack the desire and natural ability to wait, may be encouraged to even more distraction, impatience, and lack of attention span by spending time online. An article in the December/January 2001 issue of *Publish* magazine details this point well. The author, Ilise Benun, says:

> "I am really impatient lately, much more than I have ever been. If I encounter a voice mail system while trying to make a phone call, I hang up. If there's a line at the bank, post office or supermarket, I go somewhere else. I have no patience with friends who don't get to the point fast enough and, at a conference recently, I was literally in agony when one of the speakers dragged out his thoughts, like a huge [electronic] file downloading.
>
> "Speaking of which, when I go online, forget about it. I refuse to wait more than two seconds for a website to load. And, if I don't see exactly what I'm looking for on the home page, or if something doesn't catch my eye right away, I don't have time to drill down.

"Instant gratification—that rush to which our culture has become addicted—is woven into the World Wide Web.... But, it's not just impatience; I also don't absorb as much online as I do offline. What I see and read on the Web doesn't seem to penetrate me. In fact, sometimes I can't remember whether I simply browsed a Web site or actually ordered something, whether I asked a question and should expect a response or I only thought about doing so."

In recent years I have become disappointed in the obvious lack of attention span exhibited by Christian teenagers (even homeschooled teens). As I have spoken to teen audiences over the years, I have always believed them to be one of the toughest audiences you can find. Now it seems their attention is even harder to gain; unless you specifically insist that all cell phones be turned off during a speaking presentation, within five minutes many of these young people are texting their friends elsewhere, or even texting other friends who are in the same room. They can't seem to pay attention to a non-electronic source for any time at all. It is rather sad and disheartening, not to mention rather disrespectful and rude on their part.

*Information Overload Resulting in Hi-Tech Stress*

Dr. Robert J. du Puis, M.D., in his book *How to Avoid High Tech Stress*, posits that technology is exploding at what he calls an "exponential" level. In other words, there is virtually no limit to the speed of growth or the ultimate height of technological advancement. Human beings, the ones using and trying to harness this hi-tech revolution, are limited in their ability to adapt to new ideas and concepts. He suggests that we have reached a point in history where our ability to learn, grasp, and deal effectively with technology has been surpassed by the expansive upward climb of new breakthroughs.

When we are overloaded with too much new information and we don't have enough time to process it, we get stressed out. It is a lot like being fed faster than we can chew, swallow, and digest the food. If we eat too much, too fast, without giving time for our meal to settle, we get indigestion. When our brains are overloaded, without time to adapt and process the data, we get burned out and experience physical symptoms of hi-tech stress.

Another similar problem I have seen is that of adrenaline that is stirred by virtual stimulus, but that is given no physical release. When we are in an open field and an angry dog begins to chase us, God has instilled in us the ability to produce adrenaline that gives us a burst of energy to fight the dog or run away from him. This adrenaline is good for us as long as we have the ability to release it. Once we have run a long distance to escape from the dog and have successfully reached safety, we feel an incredible rush of relief. We are out of breath and tired, but we feel good. After a brief rest, we feel better.

In the virtual world our adrenaline is stirred as well. When we watch a movie or play a computer game that has action or terror, our body kicks in, giving us a boost to be able to deal with the situation we are watching. That is why children move around when playing video games—they are physically reacting to the threats being made to their virtual lives. The bad news is that they aren't moving enough. When watching TV, playing electronic games, or working on the computer, our bodies are stationary, and we don't have a physical release for the rush of energy we just received. In computer games and movies our emotions are lifted up and let down;

we are scared senseless, then relieved. This produces physical stress and emotional frustration. I don't believe it is natural or healthy to produce adrenaline that frequently without ever having to exert ourselves physically to release the rush. If you don't believe me, just watch how children snap at each other when they have spent too long in front of a monitor. Or, observe how tired those of us are who spend all day in front of a computer at work. When our machine malfunctions (which happens all too frequently!), our anger immediately surfaces, and we have no physical vent for it. We just have to wait until we calm down again (which will be a while, if we are forced to call tech support!). As Dr. du Puis says, "It is interesting that physical exhaustion requires only physical rest for recovery. Mental exhaustion requires sleep."



Children especially can receive either information overload or an emotional assault of mature information that they aren't prepared to deal with. The more access a child has to the media, the more likely they are to be troubled by stories that they hear which perhaps they should not. "Often, children are consuming information at the rate of four to six hours per day. Too little time exists to 'debrief' the children of any pent up fears the day's viewing has brought" (Patterson, 112).

The Monica Lewinski scandal of the Clinton administration is a perfect example of a situation where hundreds of thousands of school-age children were receiving the same information at the same time that their parents were. Researcher Joshua Meyrowitz says that "parents were once the medium through which children discovered the world. They could filter information, delay it or deny it. Today, however, children get their information from the same sources as their parents, often simultaneously" (Patterson, 90).

**What about Online Education?**

Being tutored and doing studies online is a trendy choice with many homeschooling parents nowadays. It frees mothers up to do other tasks, and it can provide special tutelage for students struggling with or wanting to advance in a particular subject. Multimedia tutoring options are also popular for parents who want to use technology as a teaching tool. There are some definite advantages to multimedia and online learning. However, you also have to consider the drawbacks.

A few of the advantages include audio/visual effects that bring to life events and concepts, an interactive interface that allows computer courses to hold the attention of the student who tends to daydream, and the ability of students to learn basic computer skills while doing their studies.

I guess my greatest concern about online and computer education is that it can become a substitute for the parents, which is what we are trying to avoid by striving to be Full-Time Parents. Because our main goal is discipleship, we should be more concerned with relationships and winning the hearts of our children than we are with teaching academic concepts. A computer or another teacher online or via video can, perhaps, teach our children just as well or better than we can, but are we sure that is the approach we want to take? I am not opposed to supplementing education with multimedia—I think it can be very beneficial—but I am against replacing parental involvement with an impersonal and morally deficient machine.

Especially when children are young, they should be learning their values from their parents. You can give your child a book on a computer, but it will never replace the closeness developed by having that youngster crawl onto your lap, rest his or her head against you, and listen to you read a story. Your children know you are investing of yourself for them, and that teaches a lesson they will never forget. It just isn't the same to snuggle up next to a PC.

We don't want to develop children who know how to relate to a machine but who fail to spend adequate time with their family or friends. I know some children who can spend hours at a time playing electronic games. If you walk into the room where they are playing, they don't even see you (or, if they do, they are so rude and antisocial that they ignore you and pretend you aren't there). There are social skills such as being polite, learning to converse with people of all age levels, and developing friendships that simply cannot be learned adequately in the virtual world.

### Playing God

"*And the whole earth was of one language and one speech*" (Genesis 11:1, KJV). Years ago, when technology was much more primitive, the people of the earth gathered together in a great project to establish the religion of Humanism. They had determined that if they could all come together with a common language and a common currency, they could build a "global village" with a tower that would reach all the way to Heaven. They could make a name for themselves and not be so scattered all over the earth. Their children could participate with them as they became a self-sufficient people. They would no longer need God because they could do anything they wanted if they could all work together for it. Even God conceded this point. "*And the LORD said, 'Behold, they are one people, and they all have one language; and this is only the beginning of what they will do; and now nothing they have imagined they can do will be impossible to them*" (Genesis 11:6, Amplified).

The scientific, technological, political, and economic communities of the world have one thing in common. They exalt man and despise their Maker. They have thumbed their noses at a Holy God long enough and I believe God is going to bring their humanistic plans to nothing. He will confuse them as He did those at the Tower of Babel over 4,000 years ago.

I'm not saying we shouldn't use technology; it can and should be used (by some) for the glory of God. God created the incredible mind of man, and many of the great advances made in science and technology have been made by Godly Christians. Perhaps today's Christian youth will be the leaders in the next wave of hi-tech advances. However, the majority of the companies from which we buy in the tech world are heathen to the core. They hate God and promote immorality. We need to be very discerning with what we allow in our homes.





**Media Fast**

A number of Christian leaders have recommended that, from time to time, families may need to call a complete fast from all electronic media. If the technological input in your life has been destructive to you or your family, you may want to declare a month that is tech-free. No TV, no Internet, no digital music, no electronic games, no movies, no radio, just peace and quiet. Use the time to learn to converse with one another, read aloud as a family, play an instrument, pray, take walks outside together, or simply be quiet.

Remember, families two hundred years ago lived quite well without any electricity. Sure, life was more difficult in many ways, but it was much simpler and less hectic as well. If God is leading you to "pull the plug" in your home, make sure that you use the time to draw close to Him. Turn off the voices that distract you from that "still small voice." You may find at the end of the month that you don't care to go back!

**Dads, Lead by Example!**

Fathers, you must set the pace for your own household. You must lead your family by the standards you establish and live by. Your children are going to mirror you and your wife in the area of entertainment and media. You can't hold a double standard or you will teach them to be hypocrites. If something isn't good for the children, it probably isn't good for Mom and Dad, either.

The issue of technology is so big that I could write an entire book on it and still not be able to fit it all into neat little categories with all the problems instantly solved. My main goal in this chapter is to challenge you to think about the media, entertainment, and technology and the values they transmit to your family. Examine the information that is entering your home through the wires and the airwaves. Never stop considering and praying about the voices that tell you what to think about and what to believe about what you just heard. It is a lifelong process. The more involved you are with using electronic devices, the more carefully you need to evaluate its impact on your family.

"'Tis a gift to be simple. 'Tis a gift to be free."

CHAPTER

# 10

# KEEPING YOUR MARRIAGE STRONG

*by Israel and Brook Wayne*

*"Nevertheless let every one of you in particular so love his wife even as himself; and the wife see that she reverence her husband."* (EPHESIANS 5:33)

AS PARENTS OF YOUNG CHILDREN we are constantly finding that life presses hard against us to try to get us to neglect the closeness of our marriage. There are three main areas on which we want to focus in this chapter: Conflict, Communication and Closeness.

When we teach on this topic at seminars, I often tell married couples: "Having a great marriage is very simple. You only need to remember ONE simple but important point and put it into practice, and you will have a wonderful, blissful marriage: From the moment you are married, to the moment you die, neither of you can ever be selfish!" So, if you forget everything we write in this chapter, make sure you get that one important point!

This usually generates a few groans and glances between couples who realize that, while true, it is not so easy to do.

Some of our readers have undoubtedly been married longer than we; nevertheless we hope these words will serve as a reminder of things that perhaps have been tucked away in the busyness of life. So, maybe you can whip up that apple pie for which you are famous, and the two of you can sit down together after your little ones are in bed and read this together.

As a bit of a disclaimer, we realize that there are some extraordinarily difficult marriage situations that involve abuse of various kinds, chronic neglect, unbelieving spouses, infidelity, etc. While those situations are extremely painful and difficult, and we sympathize with you in what you are facing, this chapter is written primarily for the average Christian marriage, not for the extreme circumstances. If you are in one of these situations, we advise you to seek out Godly counsel from someone who is Biblically qualified to help guide you.

**Conflict**

Conflict is easy. It is conflict resolution that is difficult! Every married couple will experience relational conflict at some point. The fact is, you don't always agree on every issue. You don't always feel like being kind or considering your spouse as better than yourself. The sinful nature can emerge in one or both partners, causing friction and tension.

There tend to be three main responses to conflict: (1) withdrawal, (2) anger, and (3) manipulation. It doesn't matter which of these categories reflects your approach—these are the three deadly sins of marriage. They all come out of one common root cause: SELFISHNESS. The fact is, as much as we say we love our spouses, we really love ourselves a whole lot more. It is only as we learn to die daily to our flesh and be filled with Christ's Spirit that we can lay the ax to the root of self-love and bring down that wicked tree and the three branches mentioned above.

**To Husbands** (from Israel)

When a man is unhappy with his wife, he tends to resort to:

*Withdrawal*—Often a man will withdraw emotionally and conversationally, retreating from interaction with his wife.

*Anger*—Some men explode with anger, yell, get violent or abusive, or go into a slow burn of passive aggression.

*Manipulation*—Men sometimes manipulate their wives through intimidation. Men are usually larger and stronger physically than their wives, and they often use their size and imposing voice as a way of keeping their wives in line and getting what they want.

"*What is the source of quarrels and conflicts among you? Is not the source your pleasures that wage war in your members? You lust and do not have; so you commit murder. You are envious and cannot obtain; so you fight and quarrel. You do not have because you do not ask*" (James 4:1-2, NASB).

The Apostle James recognized the heart of our relational conflicts. Quarrels and conflicts don't arise from something *outside* of us, but rather from *inside*. It takes two to quarrel. I recognize that sometimes one spouse is being aggressive and/or abusive in the relationship, and there can be a one-sided dynamic, but that is rare. Most of the time, we both contribute to the unhappiness of the other marriage partner. When both partners want to approach building up the marriage in humility, a context for conflict resolution is put into place.

James teaches us that conflict comes from desires that aren't being fulfilled. The questions to ask are, "What do I want? What does she want? Who isn't getting what they want? Can these desires be legitimately met in a way that works well for both of us? Can I give up what I want in order to bless and serve my wife?"



**Build Up Your Wife**

Make sure that you are building up your wife with your words. Look for positive things to say about her and to her. Thank her for the work that she does to keep your family in working order. Look for things that she accomplishes and praise her for them, rather than always looking for the one thing that she didn't get to check off her to-do list. Your wife probably doesn't get a lot of affirmation in her life, and she needs it from you more than from anyone else.



**Heirs Together of the Grace of Life**

Your wife has given up so much to join you in your mission/vision. She has borne your children, in many cases set aside a career, to a great extent given up her social life, and has dedicated herself to being your wife and the mother of your children. That is a huge sacrifice. Without your wife, you would almost assuredly fail in your parenting task.

**Give Your Wife Freedom to Disagree**

In all the years that we have been married, I have never had to play the "submission" card with my wife. Now part of that is just due to the fact that I married a phenomenal woman who partners with me on my goals and vision without giving me grief. However, I always look to my wife for her input and perspective whenever making any major life decision. If we don't agree on a course for the future, we pray and wait. We believe that Christ is not divided and He has one mind. So we wait until we are on the same page before we move forward. While I would be prepared to take the reins and lead alone if I needed to, I appreciate making life a team effort.

I have never felt that my wife needs to agree with me on theological matters, or even many preferences or practical life issues. My wife is not exactly like me—and I like that! I want her to be her, not another version of me. I am thankful that we do agree on nearly everything and that we share a similar perspective on almost every issue, but this is due to a common Savior and a mutual respect, more than my imposing my views on my wife. I am sure to share with my wife what I believe and why I believe it, but I want her convictions to be based on God's Word, rather than merely on my opinion.

I have told my wife that if I should ever die, and she were left to raise our children alone, I want her to lead them based on the Word of God, not based on what she thinks I would do. I am not the final standard of right and wrong, God is. I want her to be led by the Spirit of God and do what she feels the Bible teaches.

**Never Yell at Your Wife**

While it should go without saying, in a Christian book, that men should never yell at their wives, or hit them, I'm afraid that many professing Christian men live no differently than unbelievers in the way they relate to their wives. Your wife is a precious jewel who should be cherished and cared for, never abused, neglected, or dominated. She is to be loved, just as Christ loved the Church and gave Himself for her (Ephesians 5:25).

**Guard Your Words**

Our words are so powerful. "*Death and life are in the power of the tongue*" (Proverbs 18:21a, KJV). Some men engage in what is tantamount to verbal abuse, but they disguise it under the thin veneer of "humor." They say biting and cynical things to and about their wives, but they do it in such a way that they can always say later, "I was just joking."

"*For the mouth speaks out of that which fills the heart.... But I tell you that every careless word that people speak, they shall give an accounting for it in the day of judgment. For by your words you will be justified, and by your words you will be condemned*" (Matthew 12:34b-37, NASB).

**To Wives** (from Brook)

A wife's attitude toward disagreements and even conflict, can contribute significantly toward either the strengthening or the weakening of the union. For women, nagging is often the most common source for introducing conflict into their relationship with their husbands. Hard as it is to swallow, nagging is a form of relational manipulation. Proverbs 27:15 (KJV) says, "*A continual dripping on a very rainy day and a contentious woman are alike.*" We women can get so into the experience of expressing our perspective that we don't even recognize we are nagging. A wife's contentious spirit is like the annoying drip, drip, drip of a leaky roof. To put it in more contemporary terms, to your husband, nagging is like the sound of fingernails scratching on a chalkboard. We've all heard that unwelcome sound enough to cringe at the very thought of it. Nagging does the same thing to our husbands. Whether condescending "reminders" or a relentless return to unfinished battlefields, nagging borne of a contentious spirit produces a tired defeatism in our husbands, breaking him down bit by bit. Under the heavy weight of criticism and disapproval, even the strongest of men will suffer.

Proverbs 25:24 (KJV) puts it this way: "*It is better to dwell in the corner of the housetop, than with a brawling woman in a large house.*" Proverbs emphasizes how the contentious, angry spirit of a wife pushes her husband away—even to the corner of her rooftop (or basement)—just so he can get some peace and quiet! We need to realize as wives that the unity we want to happen in our marriages isn't going to come about by belittling, angry, and contentious nagging. We've got to get it through our heads that this approach doesn't work.

Whether or not it is true, people often say "the way to a man's heart is through his stomach." I'd even go so far as to say one of the ways to keep a man's heart is through his stomach! Good food ranks pretty high for most men, but Proverbs 17:1 (NASB) will give you an inside track to something your husband values even more: "*Better a dry morsel and quietness therewith than a house full of feasting with strife.*" The word "morsel" has a delectable sound to it, but realize this verse is talking about stale bread. Our men would rather have stale baloney sandwiches with a spirit of quietness in our marriages, than the best steak and cheesecake with strife.

It's time for us as wives to lay aside our human attempts at bringing about true intimacy in our marriages by nagging. Just look at what James 1:20 (KJV) says: "[F]*or the wrath of man worketh not the righteousness of God.*" A paraphrase, if you will, about nagging might be something like this: "For the nagging of a woman will not bring about the changes she wants in her husband." As you read through the rest of this chapter, ask the Holy Spirit to reveal to you what weapons and mechanisms you might be using against your husband, and how you can lay them down.

### How Women Manipulate

Wives tend to respond to conflict with one of two different motives: (1) to change their husbands, or (2) to build a barrier for self-protection. Withdrawing from the relationship as a means of punishing the husband comes so naturally for many women. Withdrawing only adds to the conflict; the cold shoulder only feeds the decay of the relationship.

Manipulation is a similar response to conflict, either making life miserable for your husband, or withholding something he needs as a means of "convincing" him that he really ought to see things your way. Somehow we women need to get it through our heads that withdrawal, anger, nagging, and manipulation just aren't going to bear the results we ultimately want to see in our marriages. If the death of our marriages is not our goal, then we will need to learn effective and Godly responses to disagreements and conflicts.

### Avoid Tearing Down

Wives can be awfully good at tearing their husbands down. We know them better than anyone else, and thus we know their weaknesses, too. Since we know these weaknesses inside and out, in times of frustration, it can be tempting to tear our men down in an effort to change them. Just as with nagging, we've got to come to the place that we realize only the foolish woman tears her husband down. Take it to heart, tearing your husband down is NOT going to produce the results you want. "*Every wise woman buildeth her house, but the foolish plucketh it down with her hands*" (Proverbs 14:1, KJV).

Not only do we tear our husbands down through our slicing words to them, but we women can also be pretty good at tearing them down in front of other people. We get on the phone with friends, and we know how to choicely add a little comment or sigh here or there. Only the woman who doesn't value her marriage will tear her husband down.

So if you can't nag and you can't tear down your husband, are you stuck? Living in close proximity to your husband ensures that you are going to see things about your husband that you recognize need to go. Definitely there will be times to keep quiet about an issue and stand back while the Lord works in your husband's heart, but there are times as a helper suitable you'll need to prayerfully bring up some issues. The problem is, for most women, an emotional outburst is the only way they know to deal with the problem. Add to our natural instincts the fact that we've always seen our mothers and grandmothers, aunts and friends react in the same way, and we know that the tendency for nagging and tearing down is well ingrained in us.



### Inherited Futility

First Peter 1:18-19 (KJV) talks about inheriting a futile method for living from our forefathers: "*For ye know that ye were not redeemed with corruptible things, such as silver and gold, from your vain way of living which ye received by tradition from your fathers* [or mothers, as the case may be], *but with the precious blood of Christ....*" Many wives have a way of living in their marriages that is useless and futile. To put it bluntly, they are sowing death into their marriages. You can probably think of several areas right now where this applies to your own life. This futile way of life we've inherited isn't doing us any good. Silver and gold won't release you from it (yes, even release from financial strain won't release anyone from the hold of a futile way of life). Only the precious blood of Christ can cleanse away the patterns and habits that are not helping your marriage.



We need a new paradigm, a new and God-fearing approach to dealing with the conflict that will inevitably arise in a marriage.

### The Time and Place for a Godly Appeal

Israel recently received an email from a lady whose husband had asked her to stop homeschooling (after 18 years!), and send the children to government school because, according to him, she was neglecting him while paying attention to their children. She felt that this was unwarranted and asked Israel for his perspective and advice, since he was a man and might better understand her husband. Not knowing the specific details of their situation (we don't know the family personally); he asked the woman if she had tried making a "Godly appeal." She said that she thought she had, but she wasn't sure exactly what that meant. Israel said that she should schedule a time to talk with her husband. Tell him that she wanted to hear his heart and seek to understand him, but that she also had something that she needed to say, and she would like for him to listen to her as well.

She quickly wrote back that she had never done this and was grateful for his advice. About 20 minutes later, she wrote him back saying, "Well, I did it. It didn't seem to work." Israel couldn't figure out what in the world she was referring to, so he asked her to clarify. She said, "I took your advice. I called my husband at work and told him that I had something I needed to say to him. I told him that I thought he was being unfair about asking me not to continue homeschooling the children. He just got upset, told me that he was in the middle of work, and that he really didn't want to talk about it. So see, it didn't work."

This is *not* how to go about making a Godly appeal! I think Queen Esther in the Bible is a great example of how to go about this. First of all, she made a date night. She scheduled a time when she knew her husband could carve out time away from the pressures of court life (or in the case of Full-Time Parents, without the children interrupting). She prepared a very nice meal and made sure he had a full stomach before she began her request. I can't stress the importance of this enough. Do *not* try to talk with your husband about stressful matters when he is working, tired, hungry, irritable, or distracted. It will only backfire, making things worse. In Esther's case, she actually had two date nights before she brought up her request. The principle is to make sure you meet the physical needs of your man before you make an appeal for attention to your needs.

Making this kind of Godly appeal takes time and a level of emotional restraint. Waiting to speak at the appropriate time, instead of voicing how you feel at the moment, will go a long way in helping your husband value your words. Remember, your marriage wasn't built in a day, and the pressing decisions and conflicts you need to talk about can wait until the appropriate time. Be creative in your presentation of your thoughts in order to preserve a sense of unity and respect. One woman I know really wanted to build in her marriage, but she found that every time she disagreed with her husband she "flew off the handle," so to speak. Creatively, she came up with the solution to put into a letter her thoughts and feelings, communicating to her husband in a way that forced her to deal with the issues at hand without the high-intensity emotions she felt when they talked face-to-face about problems and areas of conflict.

Essentially, as helpers suitable, wives need to see their husbands as God sees them. Does God see his faults? Does God see his weaknesses, and bad decisions? Of course. But does God still love him and want the best for him? Yes. Furthermore, does God so intensely care for him that He is not willing to leave your husband in his faults, weaknesses, and immaturity? Yes.

A wife is not her husband's Holy Spirit. It is not her job to discern each aspect of her husband's life that is out of line and to add pressure to his life to conform him. But it is her job to come alongside him in this journey of life and do all she can to help facilitate the work of God in her husband's life. Stepping back and remembering this is an imperfect man who is in process under the mighty hand of God can be a springboard for compassion and understanding for him as he struggles, and at times fails. When a woman of God stands by her man as a companion and helper in a gracious and prayerful way, she helps keep her husband's heart open to the things of God, whereas a scornful and disgusted wife is likely to only turn her husband to bitterness. Understanding that his change isn't her task can be freeing for a wife drowning in the daunting task of conforming her husband.





**Communication**

While communication is essential for a successful marriage, it isn't innately helpful in and of itself. For example, if you are still consumed with self-interest, with proving your point, and with making your spouse look bad, communication is only going to act like fuel on the fire, rather than water to put out the flames.

**For Husbands** (from Israel)

**Initiate Conversations that Count**

As the husband/father, you need to be the thermometer and the thermostat in your home. You need to be constantly aware of the emotional and spiritual temperature of your wife and children. You need to be aware of trending problems and head them off before they become fatal or permanent. Not only do you then know the relational situation of the home, but you are being a leader, providing clear vision and direction for others to follow.

One of the ways you do this is by initiating conversations that count. You can't wait until something is a crisis before you step in and begin dealing with it. You need to head it off at the pass. For example, if you are in situation where you work outside the home and your wife is home with the children during the day, then she is going to be more in tune with what is going on during the day/week. You need to make sure that you are making time to discuss with your wife what is going on in the home, or things that are important to her. If this occurs naturally enough in your week without scheduling, fine, but if not, then you need to have a set time each week where you have an uninterrupted chat. Some couples make a weekly date night for this purpose. Others don't want to take their stress on their date, so they schedule another "strategy meeting" somewhere else in the week. The main thing is to make sure it happens. Too often life gets away from us and too much water has gone over the dam before we notice and are able to do something about it.

**Parenting and Marriage Aren't Enemies!**

Raising children and marriage in the Lord were never meant to be enemies. Somehow, in our modern world we've lost sight of how these two elements were designed to work together. One of my all-time favorite quotations (by that well-known Anonymous) says: "True romance is not so much holding one another's hands and looking into each other's eyes, but rather holding hands and walking in the same direction." Isn't that what Godly marriage is really about, walking together toward Christ?

Malachi 2:14-15 (NIV) stresses that the Lord watches between husbands and wives, and that it is the Lord Who has made them one. Verse 15 says, "*In flesh and spirit they are His. And why one*?" It is not merely a physical oneness here that is important to the Lord, but oneness of spirit. Why one in flesh and one in spirit? "*Because He was seeking Godly offspring. So guard yourself in your spirit and do not break faith with the wife of your youth*."

The binding of husband and wife is supposed to provide the backdrop, the context, for raising Godly children. God's call to guard ourselves in our spirit is not amiss today. The spirit of oneness in a marriage in valuable and precious in God's sight; it must be carefully built and guarded. In the midst of busy life chasing after toddlers, guiding young people, and instructing and providing for our children, perhaps Malachi's words hold more relevance for us in this season than in any other. Guard the intimacy of your marriage; guard the oneness, because God desires to raise a Godly offspring from your union. If raising children and marriage were enemies, there would be no hope for parents! But that wasn't God's plan.

**For Wives** (from Brook)

**Stay Connected**

As simple as it sounds, staying connected takes effort and time coupled with a learner's attitude. In general, men just don't communicate in the same way as women. While women tend to focus more on feelings, relationships, and the small details that make up their lives, their husbands don't typically readily express feelings, or obsess over the nuances of relational issues. But just because your husband doesn't center his conversations in the same way as you might, don't take it as a sign that heart connections are any less important to him.

One of the ways you can learn about what is on his heart is to simply ask questions during your times of conversation about what he is doing or what sorts of plans he is making. Find out what he thinks about the global news, or what he is currently reading. Target your questions in a way that don't require an emotional review and analysis. Make it easy on him by asking questions in a safe place that isn't full of emotional barbs. Avoid entangling criticisms, untimely problem solving, or backing him into a corner where he must quote poetry to assure you of his love. Learn your husband, and learn him well!

Have you ever met someone who always seemed to have a problem? If it wasn't one thing, it was another, and as soon as that situation was resolved, the end of the earth was tumbling upon her again! In the midst of our busy days dealing with the leaky kitchen faucet, a child who simply won't listen, strained grocery budgets, and broken bikes that need fixed, let me caution you from becoming a "Mrs. Gotta-Have-a-Problem." Sure you will have difficulties and problems you need to discuss with your husband, but be intentional about infusing your relationship with lots of positive times and conversations as well.

The number one thing you can do as a wife to stay connected to your husband is to believe in him. So many men walk with their spiritual backs broken because a critical, disgusted wife never let him learn from mistakes he either made, or might have made. To believe in your husband doesn't mean you need to think he is a god, or that he'll never mess up. Don't ignore the sins in his life or call them something other than they are. Believing in your man is standing by him, letting him know you think God has put something special in his life, and that you are excited to see it grow. It is being the cheerleader for the plans and projects in his life and mourning with him when it doesn't work. It is trusting the good motives of your husband, and not fishing for every little thing in his life that doesn't match up to your specifications. It is believing God has a plan and purpose for your husband and being grateful to walk through life at his side, as he struggles and succeeds.

Daily prayer for my husband has been one of the essential ways I stay connected with him and participate as a team with him. When I am interceding for the ins and outs of his day, from ministry opportunities to success in the daily jobs of life, I take on an interest and awareness of what my husband's energies and focus are being spent on, and through prayer I can come alongside him in a supportive way.

**Closeness**

When it comes to intimacy in marriage, many factors seem to all conspire against closeness as a couple. Work, finances, activities, homeschooling, etc., all demand a lot of time and energy. At the end of a long day it is easy to simply collapse into bed and fall asleep as soon as your head hits the pillow. That is fine at times, but that type of lifestyle as a way of life isn't conducive to keeping a strong and healthy romance in your lives.

**To Husbands** (from Israel)

There are several things you need to remember about your wife and issues of intimacy.

First, your wife is tired. At the end of a long day (okay, well BEFORE the end of a long day!), your wife is completely drained from all of her responsibilities. It is unreasonable for you to expect your wife to be able to be sexually interested every time you are.

Your wife can't just shut off her day. Men can compartmentalize their stresses in ways that women cannot. A man can usually leave the hassles of his workday at work and come home without dwelling on all that happened or was left undone in a day's time. You don't usually need to talk about your day. You lived it once, and you don't want to have to live it again. Your wife is not like this. Everything she endured during the day has culminated and compounded into a giant heap by the end of the day. One of the ways that she unwinds and finds release from her day is by talking to the man she loves. She needs to tell you everything that the children did, what the dog ate, how the dryer consumed another sock, etc. She needs to externalize all of that to an adult (her husband) and know that she is understood, affirmed, sympathized with, and cared for. If this does not happen, or especially if you do not seem interested in the details of her day, she feels that you do not care about HER as a person. She cannot go from being hurt about being "rejected" by you to suddenly being sexually interested in you. That just isn't going to happen. This goes back to the communication issues we discussed earlier. Learn to be a good listener. Sometimes your wife wants you to intervene, to fix the problems and save the day. Other times she just wants to know that you are listening, she is heard, and that you care. Since you are not God, you will never know which time is which, but you can never go wrong with a hug and affirming words of love and care. Offer to fix the problem if you can, but sometimes, your wife just needs to vent.

Give your wife some space. If possible, when you return from work, try to engage with the children so that your wife can get caught up on the loose ends of the day and perhaps have some decompression time. This is important because she needs some uninterrupted time, and your children need some time with Dad. If you work outside the home, like most men, this is a great time to gather your children around you and read to them, or have meaningful activities or conversations. Remember, you are half of the Full-Time Parenting equation. While some women may not desire this arrangement, many will greatly appreciate their knight in shining armor riding in to rescue them at the end of a long day. Both of you are tired, and I'm sure you both feel like collapsing on the couch, but you need to help your wife at the end of the day. Some women want their husbands to help with dishes or tidying the house after work. While this may be just the ticket in some households, my wife wants me to spend time with our children. As a stay-at-home, homeschooling mom, she has spent all day interacting with them. She would prefer a half hour in a quiet kitchen to clear her head than the noise and chaos of undirected children getting underfoot. Do what works for your family, but be involved. If your wife has a half an hour to rest, read, take a bath, go on a walk, or some other decompression activity, she is often far more ready for intimacy at the end of the day.

Emotional intimacy precedes physical intimacy. Men can approach sex as a physical act, separated from emotional ties, far more readily then women can. For most women, they can only give themselves physically to someone with whom they feel emotionally connected to. Emotional intimacy with your wife must be maintained by you as a husband. For many women, words of affirmation are very important for her to know that she is loved by and important to her husband. Spending time together, talking, non-sexual affectionate touching such as hugs, taking her hand, or putting your arm around her are all ways of staying connected during the day.

**To Wives** (from Brook)

One of the main hindrances to intimacy for a wife is simply being tired. Raising children is a physically draining job! While proper rest is essential, don't let your desire for sleep and the busyness of life steal from the physical oneness that will act much like a glue in your marriage. That is much easier said than done. Though you may not pull it off smoothly and perhaps never effortlessly, as a wife, you need to take time to be intimate with your husband. He needs it, and despite your weary days, you need the closeness with your husband, too. Since women can more easily neglect this part of their marriage, I often encourage women to spend some mental energy preparing for and planning time with their husbands. For moms (especially those with babies and toddlers), this will likely mean a nap. I know what you are saying, who has time for that? But seriously, get your household schedule under the best control you can, plan your little ones' naps for the same time, and then lie down for what I call a "power nap." Ten to thirty minutes of pure rest, letting your mind be at ease from all the cares and concerns of the day, can do wonders. Fortify yourself with good nutrition and vitamins because you've got quite a job being the spinning hub of the wheel for your family!

Secondly, you need to train your children to work. Your children need to gain a good work ethic and an attitude of gratefulness that can be achieved first and foremost by their involvement with the daily care of the family and home. I'm not talking about unreasonable expectations on children, or unreasonable chore times that negate other important aspects of childhood. Nevertheless, it is needful for children to become skilled and responsible in the areas of family life as preparation for their own futures, and for developing a strong sense of ability and accomplishment. You as a mom also need to delegate many aspects of the daily home care because you are most valuable to your family as a wife and mom, and not the housekeeper. You need to wisely choose how you expend your energy, so that you are accomplishing the aspects of family life that only you can do. In other words, learn to be a manager, so that you can spend the best of yourself being a wife and mother.

Similarly, you were called to be a wife and a mother, not a soccer mom. If the effects of chauffeuring children to piano, violin, art, ballet, and soccer are hindering you as a wife and draining you, you may need to drop out of some of the extracurricular activities. It is more important for your family that you and your husband have a solid relationship than that your family is featured on a magazine cover as "Most Successfully Busy Family of the Year."

However tired you may be with the cares of raising little ones, respect, borne of a genuine interest in your husband, is the primary ingredient for developing intimacy in your marriage (Ephesians 5:32). Find what is respectable about your husband, look hard if you need to, and give him your attention. Let him know you are aware of the good in his life, and build him up with your words. Respect what he does right, what he longs to do, and who God is making him to be. Respect him as a person who has needs, and respect his attempts to love you. Care about him enough to set aside time just for the two of you. One practical area this will include is simply getting your family on a reasonable sleep schedule. Children who are simply never put to bed at night, or who cannot handle bedtime without major opposition, won't help you have the time and energy you need for your husband. During times of intimacy, help ensure it is positive and peaceful by leaving your day behind you. There will be time enough later to write out grocery lists, decide when to teach your child to have proper manners, and clean the bathroom. When the day is done, shut off the day, committing it to the Lord, and purpose to enjoy the time with your husband.

CHAPTER

# 11

# TEACHING YOUR CHILDREN ABOUT PURITY

*"How can a young man keep his way pure? By guarding it according to your word."* (PSALM 119:9)

THE ADVENT OF ELECTRONIC MEDIA has allowed information to spread to every television, radio, computer, cell phone and headset in America. Never before have so many images and worldviews been so easily accessible with a mere click. Our culture is absolutely charged with a sexual and sensual atmosphere.

Obviously, a big part of protecting our children's innocence is simply unplugging from the information sources. In our home, we have chosen not to have cable television or internet. Our children (all age twelve and under at this point) do not have cell phones. That is pretty radical in our day and age. However, we know that young children have survived for thousands of years without these tools, and we believe that our children can survive a few formative years without them.

I'm not saying those things are inherently wrong, especially if they are closely monitored, but I am saying that whatever choices we make about electronic media must be intentional.

### Principles of Purity

More important than dealing with externals, however, is the need to deal with the heart. Even Amish children sin in their hearts, without all of the trappings of the digital age.

Jesus said in Matthew 5, "*Blessed are the pure in heart, for they will see God.*" We want our children (and ourselves) to be pure in heart. That includes physical and sexual purity, but it goes far deeper than that. We want our children to pursue holiness, without which no one will see the Lord (Hebrews 12:14).

Holiness is a reflection of the nature and character of God. God is holy. He is "other." When we are holy, we are set apart for His purposes and plans. We are unique and distinct from the sinful world around us. Our desires and pursuits are for His honor and glory. We recognize that our bodies are the temple of the Holy Spirit (1 Corinthians 6:19) and that the place where He abides must be holy (1 Corinthians 6:15).

In the Sermon on the Mount, Jesus put a great emphasis, not on rule-keeping, but on the condition of the heart. He said that in God's sight, lust was the same as committing the act of adultery (Matthew 5:27-30). The reason for this is that "*as a man thinks in his heart, so is he*" (Proverbs 23:7). Reputation is what other people believe about you. Character is what God knows about you. Your character is who you are when you are all alone. Character is doing the right thing, even when no one will ever see or know.





*1. Understanding God's Purposes for Sex*

It is important for us to teach our children that God created sex. It is a wonderful gift that He intends to be for one man and his wife for as long as they both shall live (Genesis 2:24, Matthew 19:4-6). God created sex in marriage for the procreation of Godly offspring (Malachi 2:14-15), the avoidance of sexual immorality because of temptation (1 Corinthians 7:2), to promote loving unity and intimacy in the marriage relationship (1 Corinthians 7:3-5, Hebrews 13:4), and finally for pleasure (Proverbs 5:18, Song of Solomon). Sex is not a dirty act, nor is it something that we should be ashamed to discuss with our children (in age-appropriate ways, of course). We need to impart to our children the truth that sex is holy, created by God, and a beautiful gift within the confines of life-long marriage between a man and his wife.

*2. Purity Begins in the Heart and Mind*

Our desire is that our children view their relationships with other people, on every level, as an opportunity for them to be servants, and to think of other's needs, rather than their own. This lack of selfishness, that is cultivated in how they relate with their parents, siblings, friends and relatives, will be a good foundation for later in life when they begin to experience physical attraction towards the opposite sex. Marriage and sexuality is about serving others, not being self-centered.

I think a distinction needs to be made between physical attraction to the opposite sex, which is very natural and normal for both male and female, and lust, which God condemns. What is the difference? There is nothing un-Godly about noticing physical beauty. There are a number of cases in Scripture where the Bible itself objectively notes that someone was physically beautiful or attractive (Genesis 24:16; 26:7; 29:17, 1 Samuel 16:12; 25:3, 2 Samuel 14:27, 1 Kings 1:4, Esther 1:11; 2:7, Job 42:15). This reference to beauty or attractiveness is totally free of lustful intent. It is a reflection of the reality that God has created beauty and He designed us to be attracted to physical beauty.

The difficulty is where we go with that attraction. If we allow ourselves to go beyond mere recognition of beauty and attraction to desiring a sexual relationship with someone who is not our spouse, then we cross the line into lust. Looking at someone (with whom we are not currently married) with a desire to have sexual relations with them is forbidden by Jesus. Lust is an issue of the mind and heart, and that is where Jesus places priority.

*3. Avoiding a Promiscuous Attitude*

In Western culture, we have been conditioned to approach relationships with a self-centered and uncommitted mindset. Most people go through multiple dating relationships before finally settling down and marrying someone, and then many go through multiple divorces or live-in relationships.

Although I was involved in dating in my early teen years, at fifteen I made a commitment not to date any young woman who was not my wife. I didn't want to waste my youth in the endless pursuit of one romantic relationship after another. My wife never dated anyone but me (and then only after we were engaged to be married). We tell our story in a booklet and audiobook entitled, "What God Has Joined Together." We believe that going with someone and breaking up, and then going with another person and breaking up, is more preparation for divorce than it is preparation for marriage.

While the purpose of this book is not to explore all of the details of how to prepare your children for marriage (we have done that in other resources we have published including a preparing for marriage audio seminar), we do want to encourage you to teach your children to think of saving their hearts, minds and bodies (in terms of romantic love) for the one person that they will marry.

*4. Be a Safe Place for Your Children*

Children are going to get their views on sexuality from somewhere. As a Full-Time Parent, you should be their primary source of information. Most children get their views on love, romance and sex from books, magazines, movies, peers, TV and music. Almost inevitably, the messages they receive from most of these sources will not be Godly. Young children have no concerns whatsoever with asking their parents questions about sex. I think though that children can be conditioned, by bad reactions on the part of their parents, to stop asking.

If your children are asking questions about reproduction, where babies come from, and such, seize the moment and thank God for the opportunity to shape their worldviews in this area. If you seem uncomfortable with the topic, your children will be uncomfortable as well. Be relaxed, answer the questions that are being asked, and don't give them more information than they really need to know at their age. For example, when a five-year-old asks, "Mommy, where did I come from?" he doesn't want a detailed description full of intimate details. He probably just wants to know that you didn't buy him at Wal-Mart.

I would say something like, "Johnny, we were so happy that one day, five years ago, God decided to bless your mother and I with a present. God sent you to live with us."

"Yes, but how did I get here?"

"You were born. You lived for nine months in your mother's womb, and then you were born."

"What is a womb?"

"It a special place, like a little room, inside of your mother's belly, where you could grow and develop."

"How did I get out?"

"God has designed the whole process in a wonderful way. When a baby is fully developed, there is a birth canal and an opening and the baby can come out of the mother's body when the baby is fully ready."

"Oh. Can I play with Legos now?"

Most of the time, these are the kinds of discussions you have with your young children. As they get older and need more information, you may want to use anatomy charts, or better yet, let them see some animals give birth. Every child who has ever grown up on a farm has sex and reproduction all figured out before he turns ten. Urban and suburban life has made the teaching of sexuality far more difficult for parents.

When your children are teenagers, you may want to give them a book on reproduction that is scientifically accurate and supports a Biblical view of sex. Try to anticipate changes that will take place in their bodies, and minds, and be ahead of the game. This will prepare them for what is ahead and will encourage them to trust you.

5. *Finding a Mate*

My goal is to develop such a close, and trusting, relationship with my children that when it is time for them to seek a marriage partner, they will desire to seek my counsel and blessing. I do not wish to impose my will upon them in some forceful external way, but I do believe it is normative for parents to be involved (in prayer, in counsel, in support, in accountability and in blessing) with their adult children during the marriage process.

If I have not been able to earn their trust and respect, then anything I try to force on them will surely backfire and be rejected. If I have been a safe place for them over the years, and have been a reliable source of Godly wisdom and counsel for them, it is my hope that they will seek out my counsel and blessing on who they marry.

I am looking forward the day when I can help my sons find Godly wives and give my daughters in marriage to Godly husbands (Jeremiah 29:6).

6. *Godly Covenant Community*

I am firmly convinced that the Lord's desire is for us to join ourselves together, as the people of the Lord, in close relationship with other families who are of like heart and faith. It seems to me, for the most part, our American churches have cultivated a very detached relational setting, where we do not really share our lives, in most cases, outside of the four walls of our church buildings or outside of scheduled formal meeting times.

I believe it is normative for our children to find mates among those with whom they have lived, worshipped, worked, played and ministered. God is certainly *not* limited to geography (my wife and I met and were married over a 1,700-mile distance), however, in general there are often some inherent difficulties to getting to know one another when you have no sense of cultural background, and no life history together.

The loss of the family culture, and the greater local faith community, has resulted in people opting for rather artificial, and in my view, problem-laden dating methods. Because of the lack of a potential marriage partner in their local area, many people have looked to online networking sites, or similar methods to find a mate. While God certainly can, and does, bring people together through these approaches, I feel that the more ideal approach is for our children to grow up in a culture that supports their Christian values and virtues, and that Godly families will have many other like-hearted families with whom they share their lives. In this type of context, the process of moving from being friends (or brothers in sisters in Christ as Paul puts it in 1 Timothy 5) to marriage partners, will be far more natural and normal. The context of the family culture, and its extended folk culture, is how people were married for millennia before the advent of mass transportation, mass communication, mass media and entertainment, urbanization, government schools, feminization, and the sexualized pop culture of the 20th century emerged. Much of what we now know about dating and romance was birthed out of the changes that occurred during Modernism and the cultural revolutions that followed. We lost much that was good, and acquired much that wasn't. While we cannot turn back the hands of time, nor return to a different era, I believe that we can still find ways to honor Christ in our day and age, and to be holy in a perverted and sensual culture.

CHAPTER

# 12

# HOSPITALITY: IT'S NOT JUST FOR WOMEN ANYMORE!

*"A bishop must be a lover of hospitality."*
(TITUS 1:7-8)

THEY SAY A MAN'S HOME is his castle. I'm not sure what that means, but there have been times when I've thought it would be nice to have a moat around my house. I don't mean to sound antisocial, it's just that after a long day of hard work, or a weary road trip, I'm ready for a nice quiet evening with my wife and children.

There is nothing quite like a recliner, a lap full of children, and a good storybook to help me unwind. You have to admit, life is stressful. For some of us, the thought of adding one more thing to the mix just doesn't appeal. So, what happens when your wife (or husband) is particularly given to hospitality, and you are not? In my case, it's not that I don't like people; it's just that I prefer that they enjoy their own homes and let me enjoy mine. I mean, after all, good fences make good neighbors, right?

When Brook and I were first married, we had the ideal home. A small, quaint, country setting that you couldn't find even if you knew where to look. To get there, you had to take a county road to a dirt road, to another dirt road, and then suddenly pull onto a long driveway that wound back to our house, which was nestled near woods and a pond. You have to remember that my work, especially at that time, consisted of my interacting with people over the phone, and sometimes in person, *all day long!* After hours of communicating I was ready for some peace and quiet.

My wife, on the other hand, was devoted from the beginning to being a wife and mother and avoiding the career-woman track. After a nice quiet day at home (it became less quiet with each subsequent child!), she would sometimes say to me upon my return, "It sure would be nice to have some guests over for dinner." My assessment was that there are some people "given to hospitality" and some who are not. I assumed that I was in the latter category and my wife was in the former.

**Given to Hospitality**

One day I was reading 1 Timothy 3:2 regarding the qualifications for an elder or bishop, and I noticed that the requirement "given to hospitality" was in the list. It appears also in Titus 1:8, only stating more strongly that we must be "a lover of hospitality." The Scripture is clear about the heart of God concerning this issue. God is not looking for reluctance but extravagance when it comes to giving of ourselves for other people. The Greek word used in both of these passages is *philoxenos*. It means literally, "a love of guests."

The word appears again in 1 Peter 4:9: "*Use hospitality one to another without grudging*." That means the act of serving someone else, in itself, doesn't win you any brownie points. It has to come as a genuine act from the heart. Romans 12:13 presents a unique idea by using the Greek word *dioko* for "given" to hospitality. The implication is that we are to pursue hospitality as though we are chasing something that we desire to overtake. That surely isn't passive!



It is through hospitality that you will develop lifelong friendships, provide the right kind of friends for your children, and perhaps even get to know the future spouses of your children.

**Practical Considerations**

Although we are no longer in the "boondocks," we still live rurally. This can cut down on our opportunities to interact with other families on a regular basis. One thing that we have found is that it is helpful to be a member of a Christian travel network called Home to Home (www.ChristianHospitality.com) that links people of like faith and allows them to share their homes with weary travelers. We have often enjoyed the fellowship of homeschooling families who were traveling through our area, and we have stayed in the homes of people who hosted us when we were on the road. Many of these precious people have become dear friends.

We have found this to be a wonderful experience all the way around.

1. It allows us to meet new people that we would never otherwise encounter.
2. It gives our children the chance to learn to serve others who visit.
3. It provides unique cultural experiences by learning about other parts of the country and the customs and beliefs of other Christians who don't live near us.
4. It saves us money when we travel because aren't paying expensive motel costs.
5. It avoids supporting anti-family or anti-Christian agendas promoted by many hotel or motel chains.
6. It helps us to see more practically how God has His people literally all over this country, many of whom are learning the same things we are.

It lets us use our home as we believe God intends, as an expression of His heart of love for people. I would encourage you to reach out in love and take a risk to show hospitality to those around you, or those across the nation who you may not yet know. It will honor God and will bless you, for as the Scripture says, "*It is more blessed to give than to receive*" (Acts 20:35, KJV).

CHAPTER

# 13

## LIVING ON ONE INCOME

*by Brook Wayne*

*"But godliness with contentment is great gain."*
(1 TIMOTHY 6:6)

"ABUNDANCE IS NOT HOW MUCH I OWN, but how much I appreciate" – Candy Paull.

Investing my life in my family is one of the greatest privileges in my life. Not only do I believe my place in God's Kingdom is to serve as a mother during the season when my children are in my home, I love doing it. One aspect of following the Lord in this way is that we live on one income.

Living on one income is the case for many Full-Time Parenting families. In a society obsessed with money and possessions, where two-income households are the norm, living on one income can be financially and culturally challenging.

**Truly Desperate?**

I do realize that there are desperate circumstances. There are real needs for food and clothing that necessitate less than ideal situations. But, frankly, many families live as if the situation were more desperate than reality requires. These families are sending both parents into the workforce to get a paycheck to maintain an "above-the-basics" lifestyle. These choices result in a general inability to walk out Deuteronomy 6's instruction to "*teach (God's word) diligently unto thy children when you sit and walk, lie down and rise up.*" Why does this often happen? Is it truly to keep starvation away from the door, and simple clothing on the family? Certainly there are desperate situations, but I fear that what many of us are willing to call "desperate" is just a bad case of living for and clinging to material gain.

One such example is the true story of an acquaintance of mine who, thinking her situation was "desperate," returned to the secular workplace to supplement her husband's adequate salary, putting her four-month-old and two-year-old daughters into childcare so that the family could fund the mortgage payment of a quarter-million-dollar home in a wealthy neighborhood. Oftentimes "desperate" is however we personally define it (see Matthew 6 for Jesus' definition).

The Bible is very clear—what gain is it truly if we accumulate the wealth of the entire world and yet forfeit our very souls, or for that matter, our children's souls (Matthew 16:26)?

I respect the story of the widow who lived around the turn of the 20th century. Hers *was* a desperate situation, and with six little mouths to feed and six backs to clothe, she knew she had to come up with some sort of income. Not willing to leave her God-given post as a mother, she took in the laundry of more well-to-do folks, and from dawn until sundown she scrubbed, washed, wrung, hung to dry, and pressed clothing. She poured her physical strength into completing her job, and at the same time poured her heart into instructing her children. The family ate corn and beans every day, every meal. But they were together, and the Lord watched over them.

**What Price Will You Pay?**

I wonder how many of us would eat corn and beans every meal, every day, if it came down to that? Would we embrace what this widow gave up in order to stay faithful in our posts as parents? Obviously it is not responsible to be lazy or negligent in the care of our children; however, many parents are driven by an insatiable quest for MORE, rather than being content with basic necessities.

It is important to ask ourselves these kinds of questions: Would you give up your second vehicle? What about moving to a smaller home? Would you give up eating out at restaurants? Would you give up designer clothing, or even new clothing? Would you be willing to spend $25 a year on your personal clothing? What price are you truly willing to pay in order to boldly keep your little ones under your training?

The late Larry Burkett (in the early 1990s) told the story of a family who were so committed to getting out of debt that they went on a $40 per month grocery budget, and they lived this way for two years. That was not a lot of money, even in those days. One doesn't get any steaks or ice cream on a budget like that. If our own situations warranted it, would we be willing to cut way back on our grocery budget, or electricity usage, or gift expenditures in order to properly raise our children in the fear of the Lord? They need financial provision, but they need spiritual and emotional provision far more.

For many parents, a double income is sought not for extravagance but to try to dig out of a severe financial pit. How do you get out of the grave of debt? Well, it will probably necessitate professional budget counseling, accountability, a map to financial freedom, and embracing a new lifestyle of saying "no" to frivolous spending, bad decisions that damage your credit, living above your means, not to mention an enslaving mentality of defeat.





**Cutting the Strings**

We live in a culture that is more than willing to define for us what we "must" have. Advertisements shout that we need this or that, pumping lies into us that life is just not complete unless we have our culturally perceived "needs" (often more accurately labeled "wants") met. On top of this, your own circle of social interactions can be a huge influence in your perceptions. If everyone you know purchases a new vehicle every year, you are likely to pity yourself for driving a ten-year-old used vehicle. If all your friends can afford to go out to eat once a week, the tendency is to feel sorry for yourself that going out to eat twice a year is a big deal. Our happiness simply cannot rest on material wealth. Paul had it right when he wrote, "*Not that I speak in respect of want: for I have learned, in whatsoever state I am, therewith to be content. I know both how to be abased, and I know how to abound: everywhere and in all things I am instructed both to be full and to be hungry, both to abound and to suffer need*" (Philippians 4:11-12, KJV).

Contentment is such a big deal that the Scriptures call it great gain. In worldly terms great gain means financial gain or material wealth. Certainly material wealth is one of the avenues God chooses to bless His people, but sometimes He allows our circumstances to be such that He provides bounteous opportunity for greater gain. "*But Godliness with contentment is great gain*" (1 Timothy 6:6, KJV). And verse eight makes it clear just what we ought to be content with: "*And having food and raiment let us be therewith content*" (KJV).

If we stop listening to the culture around us, and change our influences, chances are we'll start seeing things in a whole new light. Perhaps it will even go so far that we won't see the heap of "sacrifices" we've had to make in order to be Full-Time Parents, but we'll start seeing how graciously the Lord provided and how faithful He is to care for those who walk according to His ways. Change your influences by learning about the real needs of the persecuted Church and the desperate situations millions of little children face in other countries. Change your influences by choosing to have your emotional needs met by the Lord, and not by a shopping spree. Choose to celebrate life, anniversaries, birthdays, etc., with a focus on giving thanks and fellowship, and not so much on receiving gifts. Paul said he has learned to be content with times of much and times of little. For the Full-Time Parenting team that lives on one income, remember the purpose is to accomplish a goal—to obey God by diligently training His children. There is no virtue in stinginess, but rather the opposite—God loves the cheerful giver! "*Every man according as he purposeth in his heart, so let him give; not grudgingly, or of necessity: for God loveth a cheerful giver*" (2 Corinthians 9:7, KJV). Live freely, generously, and yes, abundantly—choosing to live apart from the culture's dictates.

Another practical idea is to begin keeping a journal of God's provision. Record the special instances that He provided, and read back every so often to remind yourself of His care for you. When we start seeing how faithful He has been to provide, our hearts can really turn to gratefulness. As Matthew Henry said, "Children are God's gifts, a heritage, and a reward; and are to be accounted blessings, and not burdens: He, who sends mouths, will send meat, if we trust in Him (Matthew Henry Concise Bible Commentary)."

We've become very conditioned in our country to constantly compare ourselves with "the Joneses." There is nothing innately wrong with enjoying fine things, beautiful catalogs, or shopping. The problem comes when/if we let the pursuit of material gain sidetrack us for the calling God Himself has placed on our lives as parents. Second Peter 2:19b says we're slaves to whatever has the mastery over us. Fear of giving up comfort and luxury has kept many a would-be missionary at home. Clinging desperately to this world's stuff keeps many people outside the gates of heaven. I plead with you, don't let the love of this world and its possessions lure you away from faithful Full-Time Parenting.

When we fully obey the Lord, there is no need to fear for tomorrow. "*But seek ye first the kingdom of God, and His righteousness; and all these things shall be added unto you*" (Matthew 6:33, KJV). Fear for tomorrow is a choice, and in order to move forward with the Lord, we need to disentangle ourselves from its grip. "*No man that warreth entangleth himself with the affairs of this life; that he may please him who hath chosen him to be a soldier*" (2 Timothy 2:4, KJV). Have you set out to win in the race of raising Godly children? Then don't let the culture of the love of affluence entangle you. "*Wherefore seeing we also are compassed about with so great a cloud of witnesses, let us lay aside every weight, and the sin which doth so easily beset us, and let us run with patience the race that is set before us*" (Hebrews 12:1, KJV).

CHAPTER

# 14

# CONSIDERATIONS BEFORE YOU START A FAMILY BUSINESS

*"Study to be quiet, and to do your own business, and to work with your own hands, as we commanded you: that ye may walk honestly toward them that are without, and that ye may have lack of nothing."* (1 THESSALONIANS 4:11-12)

ONE OF THE HINDRANCES to Full-Time Parenting is employment. It is very hard to spend the time you need with your family when you are selling most of your waking hours to an employer. This chapter is designed to help explore the option of starting a family economic enterprise. There is great reward in this approach, but there are many costs as well. I want to warn you of some of the potholes along the road so that hopefully you can avoid making the mistakes so many others have made.

Since 1993, I have given marketing consultation to several hundred families and individuals, passing on principles that apply to starting and managing a home-based business. Whether you are starting a business as a hobby to teach your children finances, or as a means to supplement your income, or as a fulltime economic support for your family, you need to clearly understand your goals and have a reasonable plan for achieving them.

First of all, starting a home-based business must be something that is Spirit-directed and controlled or it will inevitably be a disaster. Being in charge of your own company is much more difficult than you may imagine. Let's look at some common motivations for starting your own home-based business.

**Top Reasons People Start Their Own Businesses**
(In No Particular Order of Importance)

*More Flexible Schedule*
There is a common perception that if you run your own business you can

make up whatever schedule you desire. This is a partial truth. I like what Bob Farewell often says, "Having your own home business is great! You have a very flexible schedule. You decide which twenty hours of the day you want to work!"

The fallacy in this flexibility expectation is that most full-time home-based businesses end up keeping the same hours of operation as any other business. When other people are going about their workday (8:00 a.m. to 6:00 p.m., Monday through Friday), they expect you to be available to conduct business as well. Obviously this may vary based on the type of business, but for the most part you will likely find yourself locked into traditional work hours. However, when the lights go out and you turn on the answering machine, many more hours of work may still await you.

If you need to take time off, you sometimes can, but those hours usually need to be made up by extra work in the evenings or weekends. You still have all of the same personal demands that you had before (a car to maintain, groceries to buy, grass to mow, etc.), and you may find that it is actually harder for you to accomplish those personal tasks once you are engaged in a full-time home business.

Unless you hire an extensive staff (not likely for the new business owner), you are responsible for all aspects of the maintenance of your new company. You are the salesperson, the production manager, the accountant, the customer service agent, the president and CEO, the marketing expert, the janitor, the graphic artist, the director of Information Technology, the repairman, and the strategist or creative mind behind the development of your products or services.

If you think this leaves you with lots of free time, think again. Many business owners find themselves working late into the night until they are cross-eyed, living on caffeine, overloaded with stress, dodging commitments at church or in their community, and actually having much less personal time that they did before they began their business. Couple this with the uncomfortable misconception that your friends may have of you (that you don't have a real job), and you will find that you are constantly the one volunteered to help someone move, or to fill in last minute for any project that your friends couldn't accomplish, because "they had to work," and you may find yourself a bit disillusioned with your "flexible" schedule.

Of course, on the bright side, for those emergencies when

you really need to take the afternoon off, you don't have to get the boss's permission because, well, you *are* the boss.

*More Income Opportunity*

Ha, ha, ho, he, he, haw, haw, hoo, hoo, ha! Sorry. I'm picking myself up off the floor. That was a good one! Okay, I'm trying to say this with a straight face. You thought you could make MORE money if you worked for yourself? Ha, ha, ho, he, he! Wow. That is too much. Olay, now that you've made my day, let's look at this prospect.

Most of the people I know who have started their own businesses make far less than they could working a white-collar job for a major corporation. You may also find yourself paying your own self-employment taxes, business insurance, health insurance, possible rent for office or warehouse, payroll (if you hire employees), and much more that you didn't have to think about when you worked for someone else.

A motivated self-starter can sometimes manage to produce more income working for himself than he does for an employer, but you need to be committed and invest yourself substantively in your work to make that happen.

*Get Rich Quick!*

You've probably seen the ads for multi-level marketing (MLM) or network marketing companies promising that you will make lots of money (thousands of dollars a week, in some cases), doing little to no work, at home in your bathrobe! As the old adage states, "If it sounds too good to be true, it probably is." The Bible teaches, "*In all labor there is profit, but mere talk leads only to poverty*" (Proverbs 14:23, NASB). Of the dozens of individuals that I have known who are engaged in network or multi-level marketing businesses, I have only known of one or two situations where a representative made a decent full-time living with the same company for more than five years.

In reality, if you want to own your own company, you need to be content to make a living, not a fortune. Yes, you need to provide for your family's needs, but the Lord has not promised to take care of all of your whims and wishes, just your necessities, and He defines those differently than most of us do (see 1 Timothy 6:8).

*Independence (Be Your Own Boss)*

The "be your own boss" syndrome is a two-sided coin. On the one side you may have a noble aspiration to be free to serve the Lord, not being encumbered by servitude to an earthly "master." Often, Christian men feel they are limited in working for the Lord because their "secular" employment (as they see it) keeps them tied to labor that doesn't necessarily build the Kingdom of God. They also grow weary from the heathen language, lifestyles, and attitudes of their non-Christian bosses or co-workers. I think these are legitimate concerns. Before leaving your job, however, you need to really seek God to discern if God has placed you there to be salt and light in that environment.

God wants to have His people in many spheres of life. God wants Christians to work in hospitals, courtrooms, computer labs, factories, retail stores, and many other spheres of life. That is part of our great commission to go into the entire world. In one sense, our employment is a means to disciple all nations with the Gospel of Jesus Christ. I'm not talking about passing out tracts on company time; I'm talking about taking a Biblical worldview and a Christian work ethic into whatever sphere God has placed you.



It could be that your desire to quit your job is simply reflective of the fact that you are a selfish person who won't be told what to do. In some cases, it is a rejection of legitimate authority that drives a man to start his own business. God will not bless that kind of self-centered and retreatist mentality.



It may also be that you are lazy and don't like hard work. The grass always seems greener on the other side of the fence. Being your own boss may look like a lot less work and headache. The problem is that unless you are self-disciplined and can motivate yourself to work when you don't feel like it; you won't succeed as your own boss. Self-government is an essential quality for the business owner.

In an age of economic uncertainty and corporate downsizing, some feel that owning their own business gives them a more solid financial footing. While it is hard to run your own business in a down-turned economy, it may be safer than having all of your eggs in someone else's basket! Many are the tales of men who have been sent job hunting after many years of loyalty to the factory or office. Whether through intentional lack of reciprocal loyalty to the employee, or simply the results of going belly-up because of financial woes, many major corporations have let down their workers and left them searching the classified ads for work.

*Dad Can Stay Home (More Family Time)*

There is a trouble I have observed under the sun. I have seen many wives who put pressure on their husbands to quit their jobs and come home. The goal is to have Dad work out of the home and presumably to be available to help with the children and household tasks. I don't know that there is anything inherently bad in this wish, but the results are often detrimental to the family.

In some cases, I believe the wife is simply discontent. It's hard to know why, and perhaps she doesn't even know. Many times a stay-at-home mother is overwhelmed with practically raising the children all by herself. She wants her husband to pull his share of the housework and training of the children. She imagines that if her husband had his own business, he could wash more dishes, or more readily help Junior with his math. She thinks that having her husband home more often will make her happy. In reality, however, that just doesn't pan out. In fact, having hubby around all of the time can create a lot more stress. Suddenly there is another person fully engaged in all of the details and decisions of everyday life. If the wife is not content in life when her husband is away at work, she simply carries her discontentedness into her new situation.

She may not have given enough consideration to how the change in income may affect the family. Please remember, ladies, the husband is not to be the help-meet. It is the other way around! Sure, hubby can and should help with household issues, but that is not his main calling in life. His main calling is to provide leadership and direction for the family. He is the "big picture" guy (see 1 Corinthians 11:3) who creates a goal and strategy for the family, and he needs his team to come alongside and help to implement his plan.

The role of the wife is described as such:

"*That they may teach the young women to be sober, to love their husbands, to love their children, To be discreet, chaste, keepers at home, good, obedient to their own husbands, that the word of God be not blasphemed*" (2:4-5, KJV).

As we have all heard, money issues are one of the main causes for strife and marital conflict. When hubby quits his job with a predictable paycheck and tries to live on the sporadic income that accompanies self-employment, his wife often can't handle the pressure. She wants safety and security. It is a woman's intuition to provide a comfortable nest for her family. Having the financial apple cart upset sometimes turns the nagging from coming home to work to the more pressing issue of "how are we going to pay the bills and put food on the table?"

Men are naturally concerned about such issues (at least normal ones are), and having a "continuous dripping" from a nagging wife doesn't bless hubby. Things can go from bad to worse if this family has not planned ahead and doesn't know what to expect. The key to this issue is being content and not having false expectations of the "good life." The good life is being wherever God wants you to be, doing what God wants you to do.

*Train Their Children (Pass on a Career)*

This is perhaps one of the best reasons to start your own business. Allowing your children to work alongside you gives you the chance to share far more than business skills. You can pass on your values, work ethic, morals, practical knowledge, and love to your children by having them work in your business. I like what Denny Kenaston says: "I don't use my children to grow my business. I use my business to grow my children!" The best approach is to start a business that will teach your children skills that they can use in the real world. They may not choose to continue with the same type of business you have started, but hopefully they have learned skills that they can apply to other endeavors. This approach of mentoring and apprenticing through work is in many ways a better preparation for an occupation than college could ever be.

While I am on this topic, I want to share something the late Larry Burkett once said about giving children an allowance. He said that he didn't think parents should give their children an allowance for doing household chores, or simply because they exist. This gives them an unrealistic expectation of the real world. You and I don't get paid for doing our own laundry, washing our dishes, or mowing our own lawn.

In order to make money, people in the real world need to provide a product or a service that people want and for which they will pay. Many parents want their children to have access to finances so they learn to budget, etc. That is all fine and good, but teaching them that they can get paid for merely existing is preparing them to be socialists, not entrepreneurs.

If you want to give your children a one-time gift (for a birthday, or just to bless them), that is fine. In order for them to have regular income, though, they need to be doing something that actually creates revenue for themselves or for the family.

If you own your own business that provides income for the family, and your children work in the business, by all means, pay them for what they do. In many cases there are good tax incentives for paying your children, and they are earning money for real work that is generating an income. Teach them how to budget, give, and save. Teach them to how invest their money wisely in ways that will allow them to earn more money off of their investments.

You should teach your children that they are part of the family unit (the family culture) and that they have the opportunity to work together with the family on household chores as a means of blessing and serving other people in their own family. Teach them why their household work has meaning and fits into their overall purpose in life (to love God and to love and serve other people). When they wash a dish for their sister they are blessing her. No one wants to eat off a dirty dish. When they pick up their toys, they are blessing their family with a clean room and protecting people from possible injuries by stepping on objects that were carelessly left lying around, not to mention practicing good stewardship.

When you and/or your children start a business, remember that the purpose of a business (besides merely paying the bills) is to fulfill the covenant promise God made to Abraham, which was transferred to us in Galatians 3: that we and our descendants would be a blessing to all the nations of the earth. You should find a need that people have and seek to service it in a Christ-like way. Use your business to bless other people in the name of Jesus.

**When Should You Start Your Own Business?**

It seems to me that the best time to start your own company is precisely when you don't need the income. Most companies don't make a profit for the first two or three years. It takes a while to build your business. Can you live for two or three years without an income? Most people can't. That's why I don't generally advise people to just quit their jobs and go full time into a new endeavor. It helps to get your feet wet slowly, so don't just dive in.

If you are not a creative, self-starter personality, you probably shouldn't consider owning your own company. You need to be innovative regarding your product line or your approach to service. If you are naturally a follower and not a leader, you might be best working for someone else. If you have difficulty taking charge of a situation or making a decision, self-employment is probably not right for you.

The best kind of work to do is the work you like the best. If you love what you do and you feel that God is pleased with your involvement in a particular endeavor, you can be happy and fulfilled even if you don't make a lot of money. I have met many business owners who say, "I used to make a lot more money, but I wouldn't trade it for what I'm doing now!" There is a lot more to your life than making a living. Make a life, not a living.

You need to find work that allows you to balance all of life: your relationship with God, your family, and your friends, ministry, finances, long-term personal goals, parenting goals, and evangelistic and discipleship opportunities. Never let one of these factors exclude the others. They are all important. God wants your life to be integrated to maximize your effectiveness for His Kingdom.

It seems that marketing is the Achilles heel of every business. Most business owners have a great product or service, but they really struggle with getting the word out to the people. The bottom line in any business is sales. If you don't make sales, you don't make money, and if you don't make money, you don't stay in business. You need to learn the art of selling. In this area you need to read good books and seek out mentors. Marketing approaches change all the time, so the most important thing is to learn the basics and then be willing to flex and change with the times. Pray, seek the Lord, and He will direct your steps (Proverbs 3:5-6).

CHAPTER

15

# A CHRISTIAN EDUCATION MANIFESTO

*"And thou shalt teach them diligently unto thy children, and shalt talk of them when thou sittest in thine house, and when thou walkest by the way, and when thou liest down, and when thou risest up."* (DEUTERONOMY 6:7)

THIS CHAPTER REPRESENTS a Biblical view of the training and education of children. Since most Christians are unaware of the Biblical instruction on these matters, I have endeavored to lay out the clear direction of Scripture as it relates to the mandate of parents to teach and train their own children in the ways of the Lord. All of this is predicated on the realization that God has given children to their parents (see Genesis 33:5, 1 Samuel 1:27, and Psalm 127:3) and has charged them with inalienable rights and responsibilities.

"*That you may tell in the hearing of your son, and of your grandson, how I made a mockery of the Egyptians, and how I performed My signs among them; that you may know that I am the Lord*" (Exodus 10:2, NASB).

The responsibility of passing on the faith from generation to generation is given to parents and grandparents. *"You shall have no other gods before Me"* (Exodus 20:3, NASB).

Evolution and humanism are substitutes for the true and living God.

"*Honor your father and mother*" (Exodus 20:12, NASB).

Government schools dishonor parents (and by example teach children to as well) by claiming that the State can nurture children better than the parents can.

"*You shall not steal*" (Exodus 20:15, NASB).

Government schooling forcibly takes money from property owners (who may not even have children) to pay for the education of other people's children. This is legal plunder (socialism—taking from the "rich" to educate the poor), and it is immoral. Legal plunder is legalized theft and is a violation of private property rights which are protected by the eighth commandment. Also, it is hypocritical that schools expect Johnny not to cheat on a test (taking answers from Billy—i.e., Billy's intellectual property), but they see nothing wrong with taking money from Billy's dad (i.e., his physical property), to pay for Johnny's education. In addition, government schools do not operate upon the Biblical ethics that insist that all charity or giving to the poor should be voluntary (see Matthew 6:1-4). *"Each man should give what he has decided in his heart to give, not reluctantly or under compulsion, for God loves a cheerful giver"* (2 Corinthians 9:7, NIV). And, while taxation is not Biblically immoral, confiscatory taxation for things that are outside of the proper jurisdiction of the civil government (i.e., social charity, abortions, education, etc.) is immoral.





"*Jesus said, 'Whoever then annuls one of the least of these commandments, and so teaches others, shall be called least in the Kingdom of Heaven; but whoever keeps and teaches them, he shall be called great in the Kingdom of Heaven'"* (Matthew 5:19, NASB).

"*These commandments that I give you today are to be upon your hearts. Impress them on your children. Talk about them when you sit at home and when you walk along the road, when you lie down and when you get up*" (Deuteronomy 6:6-7, 11:19, NIV).

This describes a 24/7/365 discipleship paradigm, centered on the commandments of God.

"*Take to your heart all the words with which I am warning you today, which you shall command your sons to observe carefully, even all the words of this law*" (Deuteronomy 32:46, NASB). Education is modeling first, instructing second. You must have God's law written on your own heart. If you don't own it, you can't sell it.

"*Blessed is the man who does not walk in the counsel of the wicked or stand in the way of sinners or sit in the seat of mockers. But his delight is in the law of the Lord, and on His law he meditates day and night*" (Psalm 1:1-2, NIV).

We are blessed if we avoid the un-Godly counsel our children would receive in government schools, and the socialization of sinful classmates, and the mocking, scoffing attitudes children pick up in school. How can a child meditate day and night on God's law in government school when God is denied as the Creator and Lord in every subject area? Contrast "blessings" promised in this passage with the "cursings" in Deuteronomy 28, and see which one you want to receive.

"*Come, my children, listen to me; I will teach you the fear of the LORD*" (Psalm 34:11, NIV).

How are children supposed to learn the fear of the Lord? Parents teach it to them by instruction and example!

"*We will not conceal them from their children, but tell to the generation to come the praises of the LORD, and His strength and His wondrous works that He has done*" (Psalm 78:4, NASB).

We should not allow the faithfulness of God in history to be revised, hidden, or concealed in their textbooks or by un-Godly teachers. Parents must take responsibility for passing on true providential history to their own children and grandchildren.

"*Listen, my son, to your father's instruction and do not forsake your mother's teaching*" (Proverbs 1:8, NIV).

It is assumed that the father and mother are doing the teaching. No one else is mentioned in Scripture as having that mandate.

"*Fear of the Lord is the beginning of wisdom. Knowledge of the Holy One results in understanding*" (Proverbs 9:10).

Government schools lack the fear of the Lord; therefore, they cannot properly transmit wisdom, knowledge, and understanding.

"*He who walks with the wise grows wise, but a companion of fools suffers harm*" (Proverbs 13:20, NIV).

"*Do not be deceived: 'Bad company corrupts good morals'*" (1 Corinthians 15:33, NASB).

Children should not be allowed to have foolish companions. Proverbs 22:15 tells us that foolishness is "bound" in the heart of a child. Ecclesiastes 4:12 indicates that a "*cord of three strands is not easily broken.*" It is hard to break a bond of foolishness once friendships with fools are made.

"*Train up a child in the way he should go, even when he is old he will not depart from it."* (Proverbs 22:6, NASB).

There is a way a child should go, and parents need to be training the child in THAT direction, not in the direction of the world.

"*The father shall make known Your truth to the children."* (Isaiah 38:19b, NKJV).

This mandate is given clearly to fathers, not to another person or institution.

"*And all your children shall be taught of the LORD; and great shall be the peace of your children*" (Isaiah 54:13, NKJV).

Children who are taught of the Lord will generally be peaceful. The converse is also true.

"*Thus saith the Lord, 'Learn not the way of the heathen'*" (Jeremiah 10:2a, KJV).

What part of "Learn not the way of the heathen" do we not understand?

"*Tell it to your children, and let your children tell it to their children, and their children to the next generation.*" (Joel 1:3, NIV).





Education is best understood as the equipping of each successive generation to train the next. This is a family matter, not a mandate given to the civil government.

"*Whoever acknowledges me before men, I will also acknowledge him before my Father in Heaven. But whoever disowns me before men, I will disown him before my Father in Heaven*" (Matthew 10:32-33, NIV).

John 1:3 and Colossians 1:16 declare that Jesus made the world. The government schools adamantly deny this. Therefore, they are disowned by Christ.

"*And Jesus came up and spoke to them, saying, 'All authority has been given to Me in heaven and on earth'*" (Matthew 28:18, NASB).

In Matthew 12:30 and Luke 11:23 (NIV): Jesus said, "*He who is not with Me is against Me, and he who does not gather with Me, scatters.*"

Are the government schools ***for*** Jesus? Do they recognize His Lordship over education and all other areas of life? If not, they are in open rebellion against Him.

Jesus is He "*in whom are hidden all the treasures of wisdom and knowledge*" (Colossians 2:3, NIV). Proverbs 1:7 (NIV) tells us that "*The fear of the Lord is the beginning of knowledge*," **but** "*Fools despise wisdom and instruction*." Despite the clear teaching of Scripture, government schools teach that Jesus has nothing to do with education, and they therefore are cultivating fools.

"*And whoever welcomes a little child like this in My Name welcomes Me. But if anyone causes one of these little ones who believe in Me to sin, it would be better for him to have a large millstone hung around his neck and to be drowned in the depths of the sea*" (Matthew 18:5-6, NIV).

Studies show that between 65 and 88 percent of all churched youth indoctrinated in government schools leave the faith by their freshman year of college.

"*Do not hinder [the children] from coming to Me; for the Kingdom of Heaven belongs to such as these*" (Matthew 19:14b, NASB).

We must not allow any influence (including secular instructors) to hinder our children from coming to Jesus.

"*And Jesus said to them, 'Whose likeness and inscription is this?' They said to Him, 'Caesar's.' Then He said to them, 'Then render to Caesar the things that are Caesar's; and to God the things that are God's'*" (Matthew 22:20-21, NASB).

The Roman coin Jesus used as an illustration bore the image of Caesar, so Jesus said to give it to him. However, Genesis 1:27 tells us that children bear the image of God; therefore, we should give them to God, not to Caesar.

"*Can a blind man lead a blind man? Will they not both fall into a pit? A student is not above his teacher, but everyone who is fully trained will be like his teacher*" (Luke 6:39-40, NIV).

Christian parents must not turn the leading of their children over to someone who is spiritually blind. Education is discipleship. The student is becoming like the teacher. Do you want your child to become like his atheist teacher?

"*Everything that does not come from faith is sin*" (Romans 14:23b, NIV).

The government schools are not teaching from a position of faith in God.

"*I am talking now as I would to my own children. Open your hearts to us! Don't team up with those who are unbelievers. How can goodness be a partner with wickedness? How can light live with darkness? What harmony can there be between Christ and the devil? How can a believer be a partner with an unbeliever? And what union can there be between God's temple and idols? For we are the temple of the living God. As God said: 'I will live in them and walk among them. I will be their God, and they will be My people. Therefore, come out from them and separate yourselves from them,' says the Lord. 'Don't touch their filthy things, and I will welcome you. And I will be your Father, and you will be My sons and daughters,' says the LORD Almighty*" (2 Corinthians 6:13-18, NLT).

We are forbidden to partner with unbelievers in the education of our children.

"*Fathers, do not exasperate your children; instead, bring them up in the training and instruction of the Lord*" (Ephesians 6:4, NIV).

It is dad's job to bring his children up in the Biblical "culture" and "counseling" of the Lord.

"*See to it that no one takes you captive through hollow and deceptive philosophy, which depends on human tradition and the basic principles of this world*" (Colossians 2:8, NIV).





Education must be predicated on the foundation of Christ, not on humanistic thought.

"*Just as you know how we were exhorting and encouraging and imploring each one of you as a father would his own children*" (1 Thessalonians 2:11, NASB).

As I mentioned previously, in this passage, in the Greek, EXHORTING means, "inviting" or "calling near," ENCOURAGING means "consoling" or "comforting," IMPLORING means, "discipline." It is assumed in Scripture that fathers are taking responsibility for drawing their children to themselves for instruction, comforting and being gentle with them, and for providing correction and discipline. Notice that the verse says, "his OWN children," not someone else's.

"*He must be one who manages his own household well, keeping his children under control with all dignity. Let deacons be husbands of only one wife, and good managers of their children and their own households*" (1 Timothy 3:4, 12, NASB).

Church leaders must set the example for the rest of the Body of Christ by taking responsibility for managing their own households. If men are not successfully training their own children to follow God, they are not eligible for leadership in ministry.

"*That [the older women] may encourage the young women to love their husbands, to love their children*" (Titus 2:4, NASB).

A young married woman's primary responsibility is to her own husband and children, not to someone else.

"*And without faith it is impossible to please God, because anyone who comes to Him must believe that He exists and that He rewards those who earnestly seek Him*" (Hebrews 11:6, NIV).

According to this verse, government schools CANNOT please God because they refuse to teach students that He exists and can be known.

"*There is a way that seems right to a man, but in the end it leads to death*" (Proverbs 16:25, NIV).

"*Therefore to him who knows the right thing to do, and does it not, to him it is sin*" (James 4:17, NASB).

"THE GOAL OF AN EDUCATION, FROM A BIBLICAL WORLDVIEW, IS DISCIPLESHIP: "A STUDENT IS NOT ABOVE HIS TEACHER, BUT EVERYONE WHO IS FULLY TRAINED WILL BE LIKE HIS TEACHER" (LUKE 6:40, NIV)."

CHAPTER

# 16

# CHRISTIAN SCHOOLS VS. HOMESCHOOLING

*"Learn not the way of the heathen."*
(JEREMIAH 10:2)

THE FOCUS OF THIS CHAPTER is to compare the Christian school classroom with a home learning environment for the purpose of equipping parents to make a well-informed and, hopefully, Biblical decision regarding how to provide their children with a Christ-centered, God-honoring education.

As a student, I was entirely home-educated, except for second and sixth grades, which I spent in two different private Christian schools. Over the years, I have often been asked the question, "Do you plan to homeschool your own children?" Anyone who has read my book, *Homeschooling from a Biblical Worldview*, knows that I have a strong conviction that we must give our children a Christian education. My desire in this chapter is not to create division among sincere Christians, but rather I hope that my personal insights might be useful for other parents who feel pulled between these two options.

## The Purpose of an Education

As Christians, we should not forget that the modern-day classroom, with all its institutional, production-oriented trappings, was invented by Prussian and socialist educators who desired to get children out of their homes and into classrooms with peers their own age, for the purpose of disintegrating the influence of the family, segregating youth into peer groups, and indoctrinating a generation of young minds.

These socialist educators, like John Dewey and his friends at Teacher's College, Columbia University, in the 1930s, knew that simply removing children from the sheltered and supervised home, where they received constant oversight from their parents, would begin the deterioration of the family as a cultural force. Children would automatically switch their allegiance from the parents to the peer group, and thus the entire "herd" could be controlled and directed (or at least so they hoped). Institutional classroom learning is, by nature, the best context for teaching the masses a particular doctrine. When parents teach their own children, it is more difficult to have uniformity and standardization among the masses in terms of ideas and worldview. For this reason the State and, in many cases, churches chose this methodology. They want all of the children within their reach to believe and live the same way.

The goal of an education, from a Biblical worldview, is discipleship: "*A student is not above his teacher, but everyone who is fully trained will be like his teacher*" (Luke 6:40, NIV). With this goal in mind, the interaction of teacher and child is very important. As a Christian parent, I believe I have been given the responsibility to train, instruct, and disciple my own child. "*Come, ye children, harken unto me: I will teach you the fear of the LORD*" (Psalm 34:11, emphasis mine). How can my child become like me if he or she is rarely around me?

There are three teachers in any school. There is the person who stands at the front of the class and calls herself a teacher. There is the curriculum. Then there is the peer group, or fellow students. The last is the most powerful influence of the three.

As much as we might like the idea (I hope we don't) of turning our children over to someone else for their education, the Biblical responsibility still rests with us. There is a fine line between legitimately delegating authority to someone else and abdicating our responsibility to parent our own children. (We will deal with this a bit more later.)

**The Socialization Issue**

Some people send their children to school classrooms so they can have socialization opportunities with other children their age. Personally, I believe that the socialization I experienced in Christian schools was mostly negative. I found myself compromising moral standards to fit in with my peer group. A companion of fools will be destroyed (Proverbs 13:20), even if the fools come from Christian homes.

I found that most (not all, of course) of the students in the Christian schools I attended did not have a genuine relationship with Jesus Christ. Many had simply learned the art of looking churchy and saying the right things in front of the teachers.

The school I attended in sixth grade only went to eighth grade. Even at that age the students were involved in drug and alcohol use, pornography, satanic heavy metal music, lying, watching R-rated movies, and sexual activity.

Their parents, of course, would have defended them to the death, insisting that they were "good" kids. I don't mean to imply that this behavior never happens in a homeschool family, but I do believe that homeschooling parents are more likely to know what their children are doing and could at the least keep their children from directly having these kinds of hoodlums as companions and role models.

While it should never happen among so-called Christian youth, I have learned that the pressures to conform to the herd are just as powerful in a Christian school classroom as they are elsewhere. Particularly during middle school and junior high, the desire to fit and be accepted is overwhelming. Personally, I don't think there is a more vicious pack of carnivorous beasts on the planet than a group of middle school or junior high students. There are many adults who still carry around the wounds and scars of their adolescence. Many young people during this transformational age are scared and uncertain about themselves and their place in the world. They feel vulnerable and don't want to show their fears, so they look for weakness in others and lunge at any opportunity to exploit it. They feel that if they can expose a flaw or shortcoming in someone else, the pack, like a bunch of rabid sharks, will attack the wounded companion and leave them alone. While aggression may be motivated out of a wrong-headed self-preservation, the comments, verbal jabs, and snubs directed at others sometimes leave their mark for life.

The pressure to find a boyfriend or girlfriend, to always be obsessed with someone of the opposite sex, and the pull to dress to attract attention are rampant in most Christian schools. These problems don't automatically go away by homeschooling, but they certainly can be diminished if the parents make a concerted effort.

### The Form and Structure of Education

Even when the curriculum at the local Christian school is Christ-centered and the teachers are good role models, the overall atmosphere of the school environment may not be very Christ-like. In many cases, the teachers may not really have a Biblical worldview. Some teachers have received their teaching credentials from humanistic colleges and universities, and they may inadvertently undermine a student's Christian worldview. Some teachers have a sincere, heartfelt belief in Christ, but their thinking is not solidly Biblical. Particularly the form and methodology employed in classroom teaching is often not based on Scripture but rather on secular and un-Scriptural paradigms.

In terms of worldview, Dan Smithwick of the Nehemiah Institute has noted a steady decline in the distinctly Christian belief systems of students in traditional Christian classrooms for well over a decade. Their collective worldview is becoming more humanistic and socialistic all the time.

I have reached the conclusion that the form and structure of classroom learning is more conducive to creating a "herd" or "group-think" mentality than it is for preparing creative individuals who can reason independently of the peer influence. Even in a Christian classroom the teacher is usually trying to teach to the "average" student. She has to "standardize" the education for the masses (or at least the little masses). This detracts from allowing for individual learning styles and discourages unique students who don't learn the same way or at the same pace as the rest of the class.

In a home learning setting, curriculum can be customized to fit around the child. In a classroom, if a child learns a little differently than the school expects him to, he may find himself falling through the cracks.

### Distractions and Learning Disabilities

As a hyperactive, attention-deficient student myself, I can attest that the learning environment of the classroom was not the best for me. My older sister could tune out the distractions of the other students and focus on her studies; I could not. Not only was I distracted, but I was a major distraction to many other students. One of my teachers actually made me my own special cardboard cubicle that stood about five feet high around my desk on the second row so that I and the other students could concentrate. If I had a question, I would wave a large Christian flag above the cubicle, and the teacher would come over, peer over the edge of the box, and see what I needed. He also grounded me for an entire year from going outside for recess because he thought it might help me to get more done if I worked when the other students were gone. It didn't really help. Homeschooling worked much better for me.

Before entering the sixth-grade classroom, I was testing at a grade ahead academically. When I left a year later, I was testing below what I had the previous year. It also became clear around this time that I had a reading problem commonly known as dyslexia. This made it embarrassing for me if I had to stand in front of the class to read. I needed special tutoring to help me learn to read, but the teachers simply didn't have time to give me any special academic attention. Again, homeschooling the next year was a lifesaver for me. Even if they had tried to enroll me in a "special class" for my reading struggles, I would have been too concerned about what the other students would think of me to submit to the help (they would have been sure to point out how dumb I was). However, at home, with no one there but my mother and sisters, I could humble myself and get the help I needed. If not for homeschooling, I would probably still be functionally illiterate.

Academically, nearly everyone will concede that a lower student-teacher ratio means that the student will have the advantage of individual tutoring and attention. It is hard to have a better student-teacher ratio than in a homeschool!

### Time and Money

One reason that many parents choose Christian schools over homeschooling is the time involved in teaching their own children at home. If both parents are working outside the home, homeschooling may be impractical for them. At the very least, I am thankful that many parents sacrifice financially to make sure their children are being given a chance to receive a Christian education in a Christian school classroom. In the final analysis, however, what most children really want is time with their parents. They don't care how much money the family makes. They want to know that they are loved and are the primary responsibility in Mom and Dad's lives. It would be a shame if parents were ever too busy to homeschool their own children.

There is a myth that children will always receive a better academic education in a classroom than they will if uncertified and sometimes fairly uneducated parents teach them.

For the 2000-01 school year, it cost American taxpayers an average of $8,311 per year, per child to provide a government-school education (see ACSI.org). The average cost for admission into a Christian-school classroom ranges from between $3,000 to $4,000 per year, per student. In contrast, most homeschoolers spend less than $600 per year, per student.

### Qualifications

Even though they spend so little per student on education, homeschoolers consistently outperform their traditional Christian-school counterparts on academic and Christian worldview assessment tests (see NHERI.org and NehemiahInstitute.org).

This is true even when the homeschooling parents only have a high school diploma! "A parent's education background has no substantive effect on their children's home school academic performance, according to this study. Home educated students' test scores remain between the 80th and 90th percentiles, whether their mothers have a college degree or did not complete high school" (see HSLDA.org).

Parents often have a very low expectation of their ability to teach their own children. We have bought into the mythology that we must always be subservient to "experts." I would posit that no one knows your child better than you do! You are the chief expert when it comes to teaching your particular child.

### Conclusion

My purpose in writing this chapter is not to bring condemnation on Christian parents who are making huge financial sacrifices trying their best to provide a quality Christian education through Christian schooling. My goal is to try to convince parents that sending their children to a Christian school probably will *not* provide their children with better socialization, academics, spiritual instruction, or family relationships. Tests are showing that the average homeschooled student is doing better in terms of academic success, Biblical worldview, and social skills than the average Christian-schooled student. I don't believe this is reason for homeschoolers to become cocky and feel superior. Frankly, I suspect that most homeschoolers are not doing as well on these points as they could be.

I do believe, however, that if we abdicate our God-given role to instruct our children and hand them over to someone else to be educated, we are missing out on many of the wonderful blessings that God has for us. Even if the schoolteachers are Christians, with better academic credentials than we have as parents, we are missing the chance to allow God to work His own character into our lives. Homeschooling is about discipleship. It is about God changing the hearts of the parents and children to conform us all into the image of Christ. There aren't any shortcuts to reaching that end. We should be willing to embrace the call to lay down our lives for our own children and model the life of Christ in front of them. For more on this topic, please see my book, *Homeschooling from a Biblical Worldview*, published by Wisdom's Gate Ministries (www.WisdomsGate.org).

CHAPTER

# 17

# COMFORT AND ADVICE FOR SINGLE PARENTS

## *by Skeet Savage (Israel's Mother)*

> *"Fear not; for thou shalt not be ashamed: neither be thou confounded; for thou shalt not be put to shame: for thou shalt forget the shame of thy youth, and shalt not remember the reproach of thy widowhood any more."* (Isaiah 54:4)

Those of us who have experienced the grief and anguish of divorce probably understand like no one else can just why our God says He hates divorce. There is nothing you can do about yesterday—but because His mercies are new every morning, the possibilities for today are endless! You can choose to live your life in the shadows as "So-and-So's Ex," or you may step into the light of His grace and stand, as His precious bride, firmly planted in the place to which He has brought you—as a joyful mother of the children which He has entrusted to your care.

If the children's father or mother refuses to listen to reason or be governed by Biblical principles and has decided to leave, the Bible says, let them depart. LET GO! Stop begging and pleading and chasing them. Stop threatening them and trying to manipulate and control them. Obey the Word—release them! Give every fragment of your shattered heart wholly to God and get on with the business of living for Him.

Absolutely refuse to take on victim status. No matter what the details of the past, the future is in your hands. From here on out, if you continue to make a mess of your life you've got no one to blame but yourself. It's time to take full responsibility for your own actions. Admit the fact that, while you may not have played the starring role in your personal little soap opera, at the very least, you played a supporting role. Repent for your part in the sins of the past and turn every bit of it over to the One Who has the power and authority to wipe your slate clean! Relinquish control and leave it in His capable hands. With God in control, I promise you, *things will be different!* You'll find that His plans for you are nothing but good! Remind yourself often that His mercies are new every morning (Lamentations 3:22-25). Determine to rise each day with thanksgiving in your heart for the opportunity He has given you to experience a wonderful new life—better than anything that you could have ever imagined or accomplished according to your best laid plans.

Put bitterness behind you and don't look back. Forget those things that are behind and press forward (Philippians 3:13,14). Allow God to fulfill His good promise to restore the years that the locusts have eaten (Joel 2:25). Get a life!

That doesn't mean you should start scouting for another marriage partner, by the way. You'll never find the joy and peace you are longing for until you stop looking around the planet for another human being who can meet your needs, fulfill your longings, and fix what is wrong in your life. Such behavior is an insult to our God Who stands ready, willing, and able to provide, and to *be*, all that you will ever need in this life and the next. So many single or divorced people leave Him waiting in the wings while they spend countless wasted hours fantasizing about some Romeo or Juliet out there in LaLa Land. The abundant life He longs to give remains an unopened package while precious days, weeks, hours and years are spent in mourning over the spiritual graves we insist on digging. Meanwhile, who's minding the children?

No matter what your former spouse does or does not do, you have a responsibility to the children. Stay focused. If your marriage and divorce was traumatic, then your children will need your undivided attention all the more. Thank God that you now have the opportunity to invest yourself fully, and without distraction, in the lives of your children. By the grace of God you can build a firm foundation under their feet and provide a nurturing habitat in which you all can grow close to each other and your God.

Don't allow guilt, or the feeling that the children have "suffered enough" throughout the painful process of the divorce (and, possibly even during the marriage) to cause you to be lenient with them in areas where you need to be tough. Many parents indulge themselves in permissiveness toward the children in a misguided attempt to somehow "win" the children over to their side by being a *buddy* rather than a parent. The absence of one parent does not necessitate the absence of Godly order in the home.

If your former spouse remarries, and the children are forced to divide their time between households, don't give in to the temptation to relax the standards of your own home in order to compete with all the cool stuff, exciting entertainments, and various tempting enticements strategically employed to lure their allegiance away from you (and God) and over to the other parent.

Faithfulness and consistency based on Biblical principles will go a long way toward establishing a solid relationship with your children that will not easily be shaken. Much healing takes place when the peace of God reigns unhindered in your midst. When just a little girl, my youngest came to me one day asking, "A lady at church said that us girls come from a broken home. We're divorced but *our* home's not broken. We *used* to be broken, but not anymore!" Out of the mouth of babes! There's no sense of lack when Jesus is held in honor as the head of a household.

Learn to look to Jesus and Him only. People can only do so much but Jesus can do anything! People will fail you but Jesus will never fail. Stop worrying. God has made very specific promises to widows and orphans. Trust Him and stand on His Word. You are in Good Hands!

When it comes to the practical aspects of providing the physical necessities for the family, always think in terms of pulling together rather than drawing apart. The "work from home" possibilities are endless as long as you are willing to be flexible and creative.

Home business options can provide apprenticeship opportunities for middle and older children, which are both provisional and educational. The children can have the satisfaction of knowing that they are a contributing part of the family rather than a burden. Responsibility develops strong character. There is no better preparation for the "real world" than hands-on participation in real situations under the guidance of a loving parent!

You may need to rethink your priorities and adjust your concept of what it means to make "a living." Particularly in this country, people can get by with so much less than what we than they think they need! If it is truly your desire to be a Full-Time Parent to your children, then you must be willing to do whatever it takes to accomplish that goal. If it becomes necessary to downscale, *do it*! If being able to disciple your own children under your roof means yard sale clothes, dented cans and stale bread, and no entertainment budget or luxuries such as eating out at restaurants (or maybe even a smaller roof) *so be it*! What a small price to pay for the privilege of being together as a family and the blessing of walking in obedience to the Scriptures!

When approached properly, teaching your children is such a simple, natural process! It is not your job to personally try to impart every morsel of knowledge to each individual child. Rather you must seek to set up a well-balanced educational buffet and then call them to dinner! Your children will need to be equipped and taught how to learn, and then properly motivated to pursue learning on their own initiative.

So, how can one person simultaneously accomplish all that is required of a single parent?

The art of multi-tasking (learning to do two or more jobs at the same time) will enable you to accomplish all that is set before you in a day's time but, hey—in the event that you are unable to get it all done today—there's always tomorrow!

Be realistic about how much you can accomplish in a day. Don't spread yourself too thin trying to do all things for all people. Understand what it is that our Lord has specifically ordained for you to do and then do it to the best of your ability and with all your heart in the reasonable time He has allowed.

In our case, in the beginning, I didn't have a clue as to how we were going to survive financially. As I began to take stock of the situation, some of the only things I knew for sure were, 1) I believed with all my heart that God had given me six children to raise for His glory, and homeschooling, in my estimation, was not an *option*—it was a mandate! 2) Since there was no one to go out and "bring home the bacon," I needed to find some kind of work that I was physically capable of performing, that would enable me to stay at home and take care of my first priority—my children. 3) After all the Lord had done for me; I wanted the remaining years of my life to count for some eternal good.

All I knew to do was go to the Lord and pour out my heart to Him. When I read in the Word that He promised to give us the desires of our hearts, I told Him that my desire was to homeschool the children for His glory and not have to leave them with a sitter while I went out and worked eight hours a day for someone else. I read in the Bible where someone prayed that God would not make him so poor that he would steal nor so rich that he would forget Him, and I made that my prayer as well. When I read that He intends for us to work six days and rest on the seventh, and that He wanted the first-fruits of His provision to be returned to Him, I promised to be faithful to do both.

I prayed fervently and unceasingly. Oh, how I prayed! My faith and commitment to everything I believed in was tested to the very limit! However, the very things that seemed like impossibilities to me at the time became strong points and, in the long run, proved to be an integral part of God's provision for our every need. Against all odds, I made a decision to hold fast to that which I knew the Lord had called me to do, committed my ways to Him, and waited for Him to direct my path as He had promised (Proverbs 3: 5,6). I was not disappointed.

Over time, an idea began to form in my mind that turned out to be (I realize now, with hindsight) the call of God on my life to a very specific kind of work. As a mother of six, and one of the unwitting "pioneers" of the homeschool movement, parents would often seek me out for counsel and advice on education and parenting matters. Over and over, I would force myself to turn away from my own personal problems and to reach out to these struggling young parents who were searching for answers and practical help on raising Godly children. Eventually, I felt that I needed to get some basic homeschooling/ parenting information into a printed format that I could simply distribute as a means of helping these families.

I spent some time at the local newspaper and quick print shop, and drove those good folks bananas by watching closely over their shoulder and asking a million questions as they tried to go about their daily tasks in each department. With some searching and persistence, I acquired a typewriter (a computer was way out of my budget range!) and typed out, pasted up, and distributed our first 32-page homeschooling newsletter.

In those early days, it was a lot of hard work making important contacts on the phone and typing manuscripts and address labels on my old manual typewriter—always with two or more toddlers or nursing babies on my lap! I would begin each day by getting up long before the children in order to read my Bible, pray, start laundry, fix breakfast, and line up their scholastic assignments and chores for the day.

In my line of work (printing and publishing), most of my duties could be interrupted at any point so I was usually available to the children and was always listening or watching for those moments when they required my hands-on ministry or input. Throughout the day I maintained an "open door" policy in the little area I had designated as my "office" with the understanding that, if the children wanted to read or talk with me, or show me something they had made or done, they could come in and see if I was free at the moment—or at least at a good stopping point.

If I was busy on the phone temporarily, the children knew that they were to go back to their activities and try again a little while later. Or, they were to stand quietly by and wait patiently until we made eye contact. As soon as I was able to get off the phone, I would go looking for that child so that we could spend a few moments together over whatever they wanted to share with me. If it was important or an emergency, they were to come to my side and whisper quietly to alert me to any pressing needs, in which case, I could merely excuse myself from the conversation and attend to the family issues at hand. Every hour on the hour, I made the rounds to check on them and spend a few minutes talking about anything they wanted to discuss or instructing them.

In the evenings, unless we were facing a press deadline, I tried to pull away from the office work and spend some concentrated time with the children. Once they were all settled in bed for the night, I would go back to work and tackle those things that required the greatest concentration along with my undivided attention, such as writing or editing.

In order for this type of set-up to work, balance is the key. The biggest challenge for me has always been to fully focus on whatever I was doing at the moment without feeling guilty and thinking I should be doing something else—whether it was working and feeling like I should be with the children, or being with the children and feeling like I should be working!!

I'll confess that I asked my God on a daily basis to order my steps and guide me through every decision I made every hour of every day. I knew that if I stayed right smack in the center of the road He had mapped out for me that I'd be headed in the right direction and wouldn't end up in the ditch with mud on my face (or His)!

Life is not *all* roses—but at least there *are* roses! I could hardly have believed, in light of our dire circumstances, that we would see the deepest desires of our hearts come to pass. For many years, we have had the blessed privilege of working together as a family to help others to fulfill their God-given responsibility to bring their children up in the nurture and admonition of the Lord. Who would have ever believed that He would bring us out of the muck and mire of the past, and establish us in such a *large* and fruitful place? Here's the best news of all—that same God is ready, willing, and able to do the same for *you*!

Don't ever think that just because there is no father (or mother) in the home the whole thing has to crumble. The husband is not the foundation upon which we build—Jesus is the only sure foundation on which to base our hopes for the future. He has a tender spot in His heart for widows and orphans (the husbandless and the fatherless) and He will be your strongest support.

"*Behold, the Lord God will come with strong hand, and His arm shall rule for Him: behold, His reward is with Him, and His work before Him. He shall feed his flock like a shepherd: He shall gather the lambs with His arm, and carry them in His bosom, and shall gently lead those that are with young*" (Isaiah 40:10, 11).

(To learn more about Skeet's books, visit: www.SkeetSavage.com)

CHAPTER

18

# WHY SOME CHILDREN LEAVE THE FAITH

*"For Demas hath forsaken me, having loved this present world."*
(2 TIMOTHY 4:10)

OVER THE YEARS I HAVE OBSERVED a number of Christian families who seemingly did all the right things in raising their children, yet their children still walked away from the faith of their parents once they were able to make their own decisions. As a young parent myself, I definitely don't want to go through all the trouble of training my children in the way they should go, only to find them turning around to head in the opposite direction. In explaining why their children have rebelled, many have refused to admit that they did anything (at least anything specific) wrong as parents. They say that their children were trained right but chose of their own free will to be disobedient. "After all," they say, "God is the best parent in the universe, and His children went astray!"

I don't wish to diminish in any way the responsibility of every child to be obedient and continue in the truth he has learned. I realize that we all make choices, good and bad, which alter the course of our lives. I also understand that many youngsters learn how to look religious and say all of the right things but have never had a regenerated heart. However, since this is a parenting book, I do want to share some fatal flaws that I have detected in many of these parents, which I believe contributed greatly to the breakdown of morals in the lives of their children.

### They Refused to Say "Yes" to God

As we begin traveling on the path of the righteous, God progressively asks us to submit every area of our lives to His Lordship. For many families God asks them to take seriously their obligation to be Full-Time Parents. They need to die to themselves and be willing to submit their will to His. Soon they begin to experience the freedom that comes from surrender and are happy they made the choice. Then God asks them to give up something else, or asks them to join Him in a certain work. If they are really certain that it was God Who required this sacrifice (not just their own reasoning), but yet they refuse to let go, it almost always leads to their children rebelling against God and parents. "*A disciple is not above his teacher, but everyone who is perfectly trained will be like his teacher*" (Luke 6:40, NKJV). Children follow the example of their parents, and if we want our children to be obedient to God in all things, we must teach them by our lives.

**They Allowed Their Children to Have Fools as Companions**

If a child is allowed to spend large segments of time around bad influences, they travel the path of disobedience and rebellion. I don't believe I have ever seen an exception to this rule. "*He who walks with wise men will be wise, but the companion of fools will be destroyed*" (Proverbs 13:20, NKJV).



**They Refused to Discipline Their Children**

Often parents say, even after their children have run away from home and are living on the streets, "I love my children too much to discipline them." Often, because of bad experiences they had as children with abuse or improper discipline, they choose to ignore God's Word and believe a lie that it is loving to avoid disciplining their children. Refusing to discipline a child is one of the surest ways to send him or her to Hell.

**They Disciplined Their Children Inconsistently or in Anger**

Many parents were not raised in Godly homes themselves, where loving, consistent, predictable discipline was implemented. Far too many parents struggle with understanding the right way to apply correction to their children. When discipline is done in anger, in excess, or simply to execute wrath on the child, it leads to a heart of rebellion in the child. "*So then, my beloved brethren, let every man be swift to hear, slow to speak, slow to wrath; for the wrath of man does not produce the righteousness of God*" (James 1:19-20, NKJV).

Godly discipline WILL NOT result in children resenting or hating their parents. Rather, they will thank God for parents who loved them enough to correct them. If you don't know how to apply Biblical discipline correctly, or if you have an anger problem, please seek help. Gain wise advice and Godly counsel from older brothers or sisters in the Lord. It is very important.

**They Refused to Demonstrate Love or They Belittled and Verbally Berated Their Children**

Very few parents understand the awesome power of their words. "*But I say to you that for every idle word men may speak, they will give account of it in the day of judgment. For by your words you will be justified, and by your words you will be condemned*" (Matthew 12:36-37, NKJV). Part of the dominion mandate God gave to Adam in Genesis was to name the animals. Adam even named his wife. In the Old Testament, parents seemed to have an almost prophetic ability to predict or determine the child's behavior and lifestyle by the name he was given. Examples are Abram, Jacob, Jabez, etc. Children tended to become what they were named.

I believe this is still the case today. I don't mean that if you are named "Bill" or "Suzy," that you will become what your birth name means. However, as parents, we "name" our children every day. We tell them who they are. "You are such a pain! Why can't you do anything right? I'm sick and tired of dealing with you!"

These comments are lodged deep into the heart of a child and shape who they become. A refusal to speak and demonstrate love and affection leads to a distant, cold, and often resentful relationship. That is why it is so vital to speak words of truth and healing into your child's life. *"Be careful. Don't think these little children are worth nothing. I tell you that they have angels in Heaven who are always with my Father in Heaven"* (Matthew 18:10, NCV).

I constantly tell our children things such as, "You are a blessing! We love you. Jesus loves you. You are special to us. I am very pleased with you." It is wonderful to watch them become the true things my wife and I speak into their lives.

**They Love the World**

Some people claim to be Christians and yet are enamored by the world and things of the world. They are fed by a secular pop culture a steady diet of worldly movies, worldly music, worldly games and activities, worldly reading material, worldly heroes and idols, etc. Children who are engrossed in the things of the world will not love God. You can't love the Creator and the cosmos at the same time. "*Love not the world, neither the things that are in the world. If any man love the world, the love of the Father is not in him. For all that is in the world, the lust of the flesh, and the lust of the eyes, and the pride of life, is not of the Father, but is of the world. And the world passeth away, and the lust thereof: but he that doeth the will of God abideth forever*" (1 John 2:15-17, KJV).



**They Gave Their Children Freedom Too Early**

There is a time and place for letting go. There comes a time when parents need to let their children stand on their own two feet. However, this is not at the ripe old age of 14. Often when teens are allowed to work outside the home, spend time away from home, or make too many important decisions before they are truly prepared, it instills in them an independent spirit that wants to be away from the family all the time. They begin to think of themselves as adults, or as equal with their parents, and they reject parental authority. Don't let go too early! "*There is a time for everything and a season for every activity under Heaven*" (Ecclesiastes 3:1, NIV).



**They Were Hypocrites—**
**Holding Up a Standard They Refused to Live By**

Some parents care only about their image and reputation. They lack proper character, so they try to compensate for that by having a good veneer of religiosity. Children see this as it truly is, repulsive and disgusting. They reject the faith that their parents supposedly embrace because they see that the life of Christ isn't real in the private lives of Mom and Dad. If you are a hypocrite, the best you can hope for is for your children to emulate your hypocrisy. More likely, though, they will be more honest than you and will be blatantly and openly rebellious. "*Do not merely listen to the word, and so deceive yourselves. Do what it says*" (James 1:22, NIV).

**They Were Legalistic**
**(Strictly Adhering to Laws That Aren't Biblical Laws)**

We must obey every word that proceeds from God's mouth. We must do everything He commands. However, some parents have created a litany of pharisaical rules, guidelines and principles that are not Biblically based. We want our children to understand what God is like and to walk in the Spirit, emulating God's nature and character. But we must be careful that we don't cross a line into judging others or thinking of ourselves highly because we follow a bunch of self-made rules.

For example, a man once told me that his little boy blurted out in a restaurant, "Daddy, those people over there don't love Jesus!" When asked how he could be so sure, he confidently replied, "They are eating white bread, not whole wheat." Admittedly, wheat is healthier than white when it comes to bread, but if children grow up confused about what is essential to the faith and what isn't, they may eventually assume that all of their parents' beliefs are based on personal preference, not on a Biblical absolute. "*How terrible it will be for you, scribes and Pharisees, you hypocrites! For you give a tenth of your mint, dill, and cummin, but have neglected the more important matters of the Law: justice, mercy, and faithfulness. These are the things you should have practiced, without neglecting the others. You blind guides! You filter out a gnat, yet swallow a camel!*" (Matthew 23:23-24, ISV).

**They Had Other Priorities Above Their Family**

"*For where your treasure is, there your heart will be also*" (Matthew 6:21, NKJV). Children know what that their parents value. When we spend our time and energy pursuing our career, our golf game, our friends, or our own comfort and pleasure to the exclusion of our children, they are pained by the rejection. Even if we are home every day, our hearts can be far from our children. We can be busy chatting with friends online, reading a book, or simply caught up in our own plans or routine. "*But if anyone does not provide for his own, and especially for those of his household, he has denied the faith and is worse than an unbeliever*" (1 Timothy 5:8, NKJV). Yes, we need to provide for the physical needs of our family, but much more we must provide for their spiritual needs.

**They Never Repented of Dishonoring Their Own Parents**

I have been noticing lately what appears to be a kind of law of the universe. In every case where I have seen a man or woman who rebelled against their parents when they were young, unless they repent and try to reconcile with their parents, their children rebel and repeat the cycle. The only thing that seems to deter this process is a parent who grieves over the sins of his youth and intercedes in prayer on behalf of his own children so they will not repeat the same sins. "*The eye that mocks his father, And scorns obedience to his mother, The ravens of the valley will pick it out, And the young eagles will eat it*" (Proverbs 30:17, NKJV).

**They Failed to Equip Their Children with a Biblical Worldview**

Children don't acquire a fear of the Lord or a proper understanding of life by osmosis. "*Come, you children, listen to me; I will teach you the fear of the Lord*" (Psalm 34:11, NKJV). Do you know that you can teach your children the fear of the Lord? You do this by the example of your life. Parents must emphasize Godly character and teach their children to put on the mind of Christ. We must learn to think as He does. If a child has a secular philosophy of life, he will eventually live out the beliefs he holds in his heart.

Sometimes it is hard to know what your children really believe, especially if they are complacent, compliant types. They may not be outwardly rebelling or rejecting your instructions, but inside they may be quietly denouncing everything you believe in. You need a catalyst or a tool to pry the sealed lid off of the container of beliefs your child is keeping bottled up. You can and should institute systematic teaching and training, but you need to get feedback. Keep open, relational dialogues going with your children.

Look for opportunities to draw out your children. Do they express the same opinions and beliefs when talking with their friends as they do in discussions with you? Are they consistent in their views, or do they merely say what they think you want to hear?

You want to really get to know the heart of your child. If you discover unexpected rebellion in your child, by all means take it seriously. Thank God that He was kind enough to let you see it so that you can pray and begin to deal with the problem.

My book, ***Homeschooling From A Biblical Worldview***, is a great resource for knowing how to apply a Biblical worldview to all areas of life.

**Parenting by the Spirit, Not by Rules**

A friend mentioned to me recently that in the Bible children loved Jesus. They clamored to be around Him. What was it about

His character and demeanor that attracted them? Are our children drawn to us in that same way? If not, it is possible that we do not have the light of our Savior shining through our lives. Perhaps we don't have that same open, loving attitude that He did. The more we are like Jesus, the more our children will want to be around us and follow us.

**Is It Too Late?**

For the parent who has a wayward child who has left home and has wandered from the faith, you may wonder, "Is there any hope at this point? What can be done to change her heart?" I need to confess that I am woefully unequipped to answer those questions. I do know that God has it in His heart to forgive prodigals when they come to themselves and return in repentance. I know that we must pray that God will do what it takes to break their stubborn will. Praying that prayer may result in incredible pain and suffering for them in this life, but in eternity it could be the difference between Heaven and Hell.

There are many other writers who have produced materials better than I can write on dealing with rebellion in children. I would recommend investing in these teaching resources and carefully considering anything the Lord would speak to your heart related to this matter. We don't have unconditional guarantees of success as parents. We can't assume that our children will automatically choose the right path. But we should not be fatalistic either and assume that the enemy is stronger than our Savior. We have great and precious promises in God's Word, and we should cling to them with everything we have in us. By the grace of God, we will be united with all of our children in God's Heavenly Kingdom.

"*I have no greater joy than to hear that my children walk in truth*" (3 John 1:4, KJV).

"While I am currently my child's coach, I look forward to the day when I will be his biggest fan. I want to make the most of my opportunities, and I truly hope my children will run well when it is their turn. If they falter or stumble, I don't want to give up on them. I believe that God will be merciful to them, to teach them in spite of their imperfections and mistakes, just as He has been to me."

CHAPTER

# 19

## PASSING THE BATON

*"Know ye not that they which run in a race run all, but one receiveth the prize? So run, that ye may obtain."* (1 CORINTHIANS 9:24)

AS PARENTS, WE NEED TO BE FAITHFUL to lead our children all the way to a successful handoff into adulthood. Unfortunately, in terms of passing on our faith to the next generation, the vast majority of all Christian parents are failing in this effort. By their freshman year of college, 60-90% (statistics vary by study or church denomination) of all children raised in Evangelical Christian homes have left the faith of their parents. Churches, and I would argue our very civilization, cannot sustain that kind of fallout. We need to learn how to successfully pass the baton to each successive generation.

In a relay race, each runner sprints as quickly as he can for his section of the relay. When he reaches his partner, who is to receive the handoff, he stretches out his arm with the baton extended, in every hope that the runner ahead will be able to receive the transfer successfully. The next runner begins running forward, not looking back, with his arm behind him, waiting to feel the baton in his hand. As soon as the transfer is made, the second runner begins sprinting with all his might in the direction of the goal. Once the transfer has been made, the first runner's job is done. He has done everything he can and should do. It is now the second runner's turn to finish the race.

In many ways, this is a great analogy for what we as parents are hoping to accomplish with our children. We want our children to receive the baton of: truth, our values and convictions, spiritual vitality, good study habits, self-control, Godly character, honor, good relationship skills, etc.

There is so much that is represented by that baton. We run the parenting race for 18-20 years, and then it is time to pass on that baton. If there is a time when the baton will be dropped in a relay race, it is almost ALWAYS at the crucial juncture of handoff. Once the baton is in the runner's hand, he rarely lets it go. But it is so common to see a team fail to handoff the baton, and when that happens the results are devastating.

**Raise Adults, Not Children**

The goal of parenting is to raise an adult, not a child. When my children reach the age of twenty (give or take a year or two), I hope that I will have successfully instilled into them everything they will need to be prepared for life. For better or worse, what I've taught them by that age is pretty much all I will be able to teach them (in a developmental sense).

If I have done everything in my ability to transfer my vision and values to my children, then I need to trust my own parenting. If I think my ideas about life are so great (that I have the best ideological seeds around), then I need to trust that what I have planted will (eventually) grow to fruition. Even more importantly than trusting my own parenting, I need to trust the Holy Spirit to continue to work in these young adults' lives. I don't want to cushion them from every bad decision. I don't want to micro-manage their lives. I don't want to be the Holy Spirit for them. I want them to learn to fly using their own wings. I want to pray for them, and be available to answer questions they ask, but I am expecting them to be adults, not dependent children. If I have raised them to be dependent children, then I have done myself (not to mention them) a grave disservice.

**Don't Expect Them to Embrace All of Your Values**

When my children are small, they must abide by my standards. I am their parent, and I am the boss. I tell them what to eat, what to wear, when to go to sleep, when to get up and what to believe. I am doing my best to bend the twig in what I perceive to be the best direction. All good parents and educators do this. We "indoctrinate" our children (hopefully into the right "doctrine").

I have very conservative standards and rules for my home. My young children don't get a vote. However, I am well-aware that when my children approach adulthood, they need to learn how to reason and discern on their own. I don't want them to adopt my values merely because they are my values. I want my children to do what they believe God requires of them in His word. I would rather see one of my children genuinely reject one of my closely cherished standards because they felt the Bible teaches them otherwise, than I would for them to embrace my view without having a clear reason why.

At the end of the day, my fellowship with my adult children is not rooted in our common standards (as much as I hope they may look similar). Our fellowship will be rooted in our common faith in our common Savior. As parents, we need to discern what hills we are willing to die on. For myself, I hope that my children will love God will all of their heart, mind, soul and strength, and love their neighbor as themselves. If they do this, I will consider myself to be a successful parent. If they choose (for some weird reason) not to live in the country, raise chickens and eat homemade, whole-wheat bread, then I will not disown them (even though I will lament that fact that they are really missing out on the good life! Just kidding!).

I don't expect my children to think and live exactly like me. I expect them to think and live like Jesus. I am going to faithfully, and without apology, live out what I believe the Bible teaches. I fully expect my children to do the same, although their expression of their faith may look different than mine.

**Maintaining Peace in the Home**

Sometimes you reach an impasse with an adult child who has decided that they cannot abide with your standards for your household. They may have planted their feet, and will not comply with your need to govern your own household. Sometimes this can create tension, especially if you have younger children for whom you are still accountable. Perhaps the younger children are embracing the views of their older siblings, and are prematurely attempting to exert their independence. In those situations, it may be necessary to have a parting of ways between that adult child and the rest of your household. Hopefully this doesn't need to be a bloody battle. Ideally, this can simply be a mutual understanding that you are no longer able to live together in a mutually compatible arrangement.

I don't believe that this parting needs to be viewed as either inevitable with every child at some arbitrary age, or as a relational failure. It may simply be a necessary part of the baton passing process.

The parent can affirm the adult child's right to make his or her own decisions (like having cable television for example), and the adult child should recognize his parents' desire (and right) not to have it in their home. Hopefully, this can be worked out in a manner that is conducive to all parties.

The adult child may just need to find his or her own place to live. Again, I don't have easy solutions on all of these issues. I trust God to give you grace and wisdom if you reach such an impasse. I also hope that you have mutually respected Christian friends or church leaders who can help to provide Godly wisdom and counsel for your family in these matters.



### Passing the Baton

As I am running toward my child, trying to pass on my faith and values, I don't want to let go of the baton too soon. I want to ensure that my child is in motion, arm extended, ready to receive it. I want to be certain that he has firmly grasped the handoff before I let go.

However, when I *do* let go, I want to genuinely *let go*. I don't want to run around the track, hanging on to the baton so that my child won't drop it! I don't want to run alongside her, yelling instructions about how to run the race. Instead, I want to catch my breath and cheer her on. If she starts to run off-track, I will send up a prayer and trust that all the training I've given her will pay off. I will trust that she will quickly regain her view of the finish line and renew her stride.



While I am currently my child's coach, I look forward to the day when I will be his biggest fan. I want to make the most of my opportunities, and I truly hope my children will run well when it is their turn. If they falter or stumble, I don't want to give up on them. I believe that God will be merciful to them, to teach them in spite of their imperfections and mistakes, just as He has been to me. I don't care if his running style is different than mine, what is important is that we are on the same team (assuming this is the case) and that we will someday both receive the prize for having run well.

My hope and prayer for all Christian parents is that they will be successful in transferring what *really* matters (a love for the Lord and others), and will be willing to let go of the things that aren't essential. May the Lord grant us grace to be gracious to one another, and successfully pass on the baton, not merely from one generation to the next, but from generation, to generation, to the next generation, and so on, for the glory of God.

CHAPTER

# 20

# PARENTING BY GRACE

*"Therefore it is of faith, that it might be by grace."*
(ROMANS 14:6)

I WAS SITTING ON THE PLATFORM of a Christian parenting conference looking out over the audience. This was one of those end-of-the day Q&A sessions where all of the exhausted main speakers field questions and try to think on their feet. One of the other speakers had the microphone and was replying to a question by waxing eloquent about the wonderful virtues of fathers being leaders in their homes.

His general synopsis was that if dads would not get involved in leading their wives and children and take seriously their responsibility to raise their own children, we could expect to see an entire generation of young people go off the deep-end spiritually and morally. He cited statistics of what happens to young people who are raised in homes where the dad is not actively involved in their lives. He raised the issue of the breakdown of the American family and how divorce was wreaking havoc on young lives. He stated how children are much more likely to be involved in violent crime, experience unwed pregnancies, experience domestic abuse in their marriages, get divorced themselves, and on and on, if the parents are divorced and/or the father is not actively leading the family.

It was a rather surreal moment for me. Knowing that the microphone would soon be passed to me for my comment, my head was spinning. I found myself wanting to nod my head in approval and shake it in protest all at the same time. On the one hand, he was so right.

As I mentioned previously, as a chaplain in the juvenile justice system I've asked about 300 young men about their relationships with their fathers.

Most of the time they never knew their dads, or their fathers were completely absent from their lives. I only remember one or two cases where a young inmate said he had a good relationship with his father (and those were first-time minor incident offenders). I heard just this morning on the radio that 70 percent of all juvenile offenders have had no positive involvement from their fathers at all. The facts seem clear to me that young men with proactive fathers just don't end up in juvenile crime. He was so right.

In spite of my general agreement, another part of me felt really awkward. If this view was correct (that without a Godly father in the home, children are doomed to languish in spiritual lethargy and/or moral decadence) how could I explain my situation?

My parents divorced when I was six. My mother, who was not a Christian at the time, remarried, and I lived with a very physically abusive stepfather for the next nine years, until he found someone else and moved on with his life. We were not exactly the poster family for Godly Full-Time Parenting! I could identify experientially with everything the other speaker was saying. At fifteen years of age, I too was becoming a statistic. I was becoming angry, violent, and bitter. Our family was a mess and getting worse all the time.

Even though we were being homeschooled, it didn't solve all of life's problems. "So," I thought, "I guess the other speaker is right. Without a good dad in the home, you are just up creek without a paddle."

Something kept nagging at me, though, as I listened. "He's forgetting something," I thought to myself. Then it hit me. I could sum up in one word what was missing from his worldview. "Grace."

When I was twelve, my mother met God. She wasn't out looking for Him. He just intervened in her life in an amazing and powerfully transformational way. Her "Damascus Road" experience was enough to get the attention of myself and my five sisters. I've never seen anyone get as sold out to Jesus as my mom did. She's still the most radical Christian I know (after nearly 25 years!). When she met Jesus we were living in poverty, fear, and defeat. We had been through welfare, battered-women shelters, and homelessness. We knew what it was like to be dysfunctional. We had no idea what it meant to be a Godly family. Even churches didn't want us showing up for services because we made them look bad.

Now, so many years later, I hardly recognize us as the same people. The difference is 180 degrees. The fact that God has seen fit, in His divine providence (and sense of humor), to give us a national ministry to families is beyond comprehension.

In God's great mercy and kindness, He allowed my wife Brook and me to start our marriage off on the right foot. We had a clean slate and have had no regrets in our marriage. We have seven beautiful children (so far) who bless us every day. We are excited about teaching and training them in the ways of the Lord. We are blessed that we get to teach other people the Biblical principles that we have learned about Godly family relationships. I'm spoiled rotten.

I can trace all of these covenant blessings back to one decision, and it wasn't mine. My mother, looking at the prospect of raising six children all alone, with no husband and no financial security, decided to trust God with her whole heart. Proverbs 3:5-7 are verses that she has lived out consistently. Everything that I have received in my life from the hand of God began initially as the result of her faith. My mother humbled herself and received God's grace (James 4:6).

We found God to be the husband to the widow and the father to the fatherless (Psalm 68:5). God proved Himself to be sufficient for us in every way. Those that honor God will be honored by Him (1 Samuel 2:30). My mother had nothing going for her except the fact that she trusted God completely. She hadn't even finished ninth grade! She had no job skills and no means for making a living. When she became a single parent, we didn't even own a car! We had no chance at all of making anything of our lives. There was only one word that stood between us and utter ruin: Grace.

When God intervenes in a situation, He does the impossible. He uses the foolish things of this world to confound the wise. He uses the weak things of this world to confuse the strong. He can take a family that is messed up, full of bad choices and mistakes, and He can make something beautiful of all the mess. It just takes absolute surrender. It takes throwing yourself on the mercy of God. It takes giving up and refusing to try to run your life one day longer. It means letting Christ take control of every facet of your existence. He wants complete, total, and final Lordship of everything that you are.

Now don't get me wrong. I'm not down on men taking leadership in their homes. Because of what I've lived through, I think I am way more intentional about taking my place as head of my home than most other men I know! I'm intense about fathers leading their children in family worship and being

Godly role models. I'm all about Malachi 4:6 and seeing fathers turn their hearts to their children.

What I've learned, however, is that if God uses a man to lead his family in paths of righteousness, and his children learn to walk in truth through his instruction and nurture, that is a work of grace. If God raises up a generation of men who are not going to wimp out like the generations before them (and I see this happening all over the country!), that is a work of grace. If the Christian community is carried into the next generation on the shoulders of Godly men who love their families and lay down their lives for their wives and children, that is a work of grace.

The point is, it really isn't about us as fathers, at least not ultimately. It's all about grace.

It isn't about faithful single parents who lead their children as the lone sanctifying spouse. It isn't about Christian mothers trying to do their best while living with abusive, ambivalent or non-Christian husbands. It's all about grace.

As much as I love my mother and thank God for her faithful example, it really isn't about her. It's all about grace!

Anything good that we have in life is an undeserved gift from God's hand. The way we avail ourselves of that grace is through humility. We have to come to the end of our rope and admit that there is a God, and we are not He. When we are finally broken and surrendered to His will alone, He will raise us up. Whether you are a single parent or a faithful Bible-teaching, patriarchal leader of your home, it isn't ultimately about you. It's all about God and His marvelous grace. Throw yourself on the merits of Christ and watch in amazement what He can do in and through you and your family.